# TAX
## HANDBOOK
## 2010/11

"Tax need not be taxing if you follow these golden rules: read this book, keep paperwork in good order, and don't leave it to the last minute – allow yourself plenty of time."

Tony Levene

**About the author**
Tony Levene has been a financial writer for over three decades specialising in personal finance. He has worked for a number of national newspapers, including the *Sunday Times* and *Daily Express*. He is the author of several books including *How to Win in the Insurance Jungle*, *The Shares Game* and *Investing for Dummies*. Tony worked for *The Guardian* from 1998 to 2009 and was voted Consumer Champion 2008 by headlinemoney.co.uk and awarded the Lifetime Achievement award by the Association of British Insurers in 2009. Tony lives in London with Claudia, grown-up children Zoë and Oliver, and cats Plato, Pandora and Pascal.

You can access free tax updates at
www.which.co.uk/taxhandbook

# TAX
## HANDBOOK
## 2010/11

TONY LEVENE

Which? Books are commissioned and published by Which? Ltd,
2 Marylebone Road, London NW1 4DF
Email: books@which.co.uk

Distributed by Littlehampton Book Services Ltd, Faraday Close, Durrington, Worthing,
West Sussex BN13 3RB

British Library Cataloguing in Publication Data
A catalogue record for this book is available from the British Library

First edition 2007
Second edition 2008
Third edition 2009
Fourth edition 2010

Copyright ©Which? Ltd 2007, 2008, 2009, 2010

ISBN 978 1 84490 104 3

1 3 5 7 9 10 8 6 4 2

Although the author and publishers endeavour to make sure the information
in this book is accurate and up-to-date, it is only a general guide. Before taking action
on financial, legal, or medical matters you should consult a qualified professional
adviser, who can consider your individual circumstances. The author and publishers can
not accordingly accept liability for any loss or damage suffered as a consequence of
relying on the information contained in this guide.

**Publisher's acknowledgements**
The publishers would like to thank Leonie Kerswill at PricewaterhouseCoopers LLP and
Ian Robinson and Teresa Fritz at Which? for their comments on the manuscript.

Senior Editor: Katy Denny
Edited by Emma Callery
Designed by Bob Vickers
Index by Lynda Swindells
Printed and bound by: Charterhouse, Hatfield

Arctic Volume White is an elemental chlorine-free paper produced at Arctic Paper
Hafrestroms AB in Åsensbruk, Sweden, using timber from sustainably managed
forests. The mill is ISO14001 and EMAS certified, and has FSC certified Chain of
Custody.

For a full list of Which? Books, please call 01903 828557, access our website at
www.which.co.uk, or write to Littlehampton Book Services.
For other enquiries call 0800 252 100.

# Contents

# Introduction

Mention the word 'tax' to most people and their first - and often - only reaction is to ask for ways they can cut their tax bill. But once you ask those self same people if they want cuts in education, the national health service, road building or local street cleaning and their response is almost invariably 'no'.

That, in a nutshell, is the problem. We want to pay less as individuals but generally we want more (or at least not less) in state-provided services. Other than mortgaging all our futures with huge borrowings, there is no easy way to square this circle. While we can all come up with taxes we think are unfair from our own perspectives, or which fall predominantly on one group or another, you cannot escape the fact that, as Benjamin Franklin said in 1789, 'In this world, nothing can be said to be certain, except death and taxes.'

Tax affects everybody, and here are some of the ways it can affect you:

- **The non-taxpayer** needs to know how to reclaim tax deducted from their savings interest.
- **The person living on a low income** needs to know about claiming Tax and Pension Credits.
- **Those on middling incomes** need to work their way through a confusing – and often changing – set of rules (and some rewards).
- **Even those on the highest incomes** employing the priciest accountants and

tax lawyers – they can charge more per minute than this book costs – still need to know about tax because they have to sign their own tax forms themselves and therefore the ultimate responsibility rests with them.

## GOVERNMENT RESOURCES

Her Majesty's Revenue & Customs (HMRC) is the Government department charged both with most forms of tax raising and with returning some of the cash to the lower paid via credits. It comprises what was formerly the Inland Revenue, Customs & Excise and National Insurance.

These departments do not, as yet, operate as a seamless whole. Nor is there any 'big bang' date when everything will become a one-stop shop, although the website (see opposite) does cover all its varied tax-gathering activities. But while there might well be well-publicised glitches, HMRC is undoubtedly becoming better at its job, which is to ensure that each one of us pays (or claims) exactly the right amount. In addition, as HMRC has become increasingly automated, so it has left

# Using the HMRC website

The HMRC website – www.hmrc.gov.uk – is referred to often in this book. It offers a comprehensive array of information with everything from the latest press release on a 'phishing' scam designed by criminals but pretending to come from HMRC to huge discussion papers, published to give all interested parties the chance to see the thinking of those at the top of the organisation. At the same time, it also has everything from the most basic leaflet for the first-time taxpayer (nearly all are downloadable as PDF files), via what you can bring back through customs from overseas to Information that only hardened tax professionals will need – let alone claim to understand.

But no one can pretend that navigating the present site (much of which is also available in Welsh) is always easy or consumer friendly. Here are some hints to help you on your way.

## Search via the home page rather than the search facility on the site

The home page leads to other pages, which tell you how to register for online self-assessment or how to check if a charity is for real. Click on 'individuals and employees' and you will find most of the self-assessment forms you will need (watch out – sometimes initials replace words, so SA means self-assessment). You will also find a mix of information ranging from National Insurance (useful for most) to the accrued income scheme (it helps you work out your tax if you buy or sell certain interest-bearing bonds).

## Make use of the tabs

Those for 'do it online' and 'quick links' lead to more specific areas.

## Use the site map

Wherever you are on the site, you can quickly return to the site map (see the tabs at the top of the website), which can be very useful.

## Explore 'Your frequently asked questions'

There is also a link to 'Your frequently asked questions', which divides the frequently asked questions into subject-related groups.

## Whatever information you are looking for, be patient!

The website has improved and it will improve further. In the meantime, warts and all, the website does have almost everything anyone will ever need.

its human resources more time to catch the dodgers whose tax the rest of us have to pay. This is to be welcomed.

## WHAT'S NEW THIS YEAR?

The main story to emerge from the Budget in 2010 is the start of a new squeeze on the taxpayer – one that is set to go on for several years. This is manifested in the lack of change in any of the main tax relief levels. Personal allowances and the level at which various tax rates start are usually upgraded at least in line with rising prices. This time, they remained set in stone. Economists call this "fiscal drag".

So the effect will be more dragged into the tax net at the low end of the earnings scale. Even those who earn too little to pay income tax may be dragged into paying National Insurance, if they work occasional weeks, although someone in this position will find their payments are little use in building up a National Insurance record.

More are now liable to pay income tax at 40 per cent instead of 20 per cent because they will slip over the line.

For very high earners – those making over £150,000 – there is the new 50 per cent tax rate which the government has dubbed "additional rate". The 40 per cent rate is no longer the top rate – it's now called the "higher rate".

To make matters worse for high earners, the personal allowance – the first slice of income that is tax free – is to be progressively withdrawn from those earning over £100,000.

The planned increase in the tax free element of Inheritance Tax to £350,000 has been cancelled.

## WHAT'S COMING FOR 2011?

More squeezing of taxpayers. National Insurance is due to rise one per cent across the board. Employees will pay 12 per cent instead of 11 per cent, the "surcharge" on higher incomes is due to rise from one to two per cent while employers also have to pay one per cent more at 13.8 per cent.

Tax relief on pensions bought by those earning more than £150,000 will also be reduced.

And there will be a new 5 per cent stamp duty rate on properties topping £1 million.

All this could change – for the better or for the worse – as no government is bound to follow a previous budget.

For updates on tax changes from May 2010 visit www.which.co.uk/taxhandbook.

# Taxes and taxing

The Treasury raises money from individuals in many different ways, ranging from taxing income to taxing alcohol. This chapter looks at the basics of each – how they are raised, how much you have to pay and whether you could pay less.

# Income Tax

This tax is at the very heart of the system, and the most significant tax for individuals both in terms of money raised and the amount of effort needed to stay on top of it and pay the correct amount.

Income Tax is the only central government tax that everyone has to consider on an annual basis – whether to work out how much to pay, to calculate if there is a potential tax rebate or to find out if they can apply for a Tax Credit, which will boost their income. It is a cradle to grave tax and if you don't earn much, you may be able to reclaim tax or gain a Tax Credit.

Income Tax is calculated on everything you earn. This includes your:

- Salary or wages
- Bonuses
- Commissions and tips
- Pension (whether paid by your former employer or an insurance company)
- Earnings from self-employment and many sources of spare time earnings
- Interest from most forms of savings accounts
- Dividends from stocks and shares (both UK and foreign)
- Dividends from open-ended investment companies (more usually known as unit trusts)
- Rental income from almost all types of landlord activity, including buy to let
- Earnings from abroad, including anything you earn by renting out holiday homes.

## ALLOWANCES AND DEDUCTIONS

Once taxpayers have added up their income in all the categories that apply to them, they can then start to subtract certain amounts. Every taxpayer, no matter what age they might be (and everyone is a potential taxpayer from the day they are born), has a **Personal Allowance**. This is set each year – for 2010–11 it is £6,475.

### Age allowances

If you are aged 65–74, your tax allowance for 2010–11 is £9,490, and if you are 75 or over, then your allowance is higher again at £9,640. However, 'enhanced' age-related allowance (over and above the basic Personal Allowance) is restricted where your income exceeds a certain level. Once your income has passed this level, the 'enhanced' age allowance (whether for 65 to 74 or the 75-plus age group) starts to erode until it reaches a higher level where it disappears altogether for that year.

**❝ Income Tax is calculated on everything that you earn. ❞**

## Other allowances

Some older people may also receive a further allowance for being married, although this is given as a Tax Credit in the tax computation (see page 28). Furthermore, there is an additional allowance for registered blind people. If all these allowances taken together are equal to – or are higher than – your earnings, then you pay no Income Tax for that year.

## Further deductions

As well as your allowances, there are other deductions you can make from your income. There are several, but the most significant are pension contributions you make to a company pension scheme and gifts of assets made to a charity.

Once your allowances have been taken away from your earnings, the figure that is left is known as your **net income** or your **taxable income**. This is the basis of the calculation.

The current system charges the first slice of your taxable income at 20 per cent, while the balance, if any, is charged firstly at 40 per cent and then at 50 per cent (see the table, overleaf, for the 2010–11 'threshold figures', which show when you move from one rate to the next). Dividends are taxable at 10 per cent, unless they fall within the higher-rate band, when they are taxable

**" Once your allowances have been taken away from your earnings, the figure that is left is known as your net income. "**

### Age allowance limits 2010-11

| Age | Lower limit | Upper limit |
| --- | --- | --- |
| 65-74 | £22,900 | £28,930 |
| 75+ | £22,900 | £29,230 |

## Tax bands at a glance (2010-11 tax year)

| Percentage of tax paid | Tax band | Cash break | Threshold |
|---|---|---|---|
| 0% | Tax-free Personal Allowance | First £6,475 of taxable income you receive | £6,475 |
| 20% | Basic rate | Next £37,400 | £43,875 |
| 40% | Higher rate | Next £112,600 | £150,000 |
| 50% | Additional rate | Remainder | – |

at 32.5 per cent, instead of 40 per cent. Anyone on the 50 per cent "additional" rate pays 42.5 per cent on dividend income. On top of this, most taxpayers have to pay National Insurance contributions on their earnings from work (see pages 15–16).

Although most people pay the majority of their Income Tax through their salary or wage packet monthly or weekly – this is known as Pay As You Earn or PAYE – your personal Income Tax liability is computed once a year. Most taxpayers need do nothing more than ensure the PAYE sums are right. Employers use tables, now usually electronic, from Her Majesty's Revenue & Customs (HMRC) to work out the tax. Your employer or pension provider will

take tax from your earnings according to your **tax code** (see pages 26–33). It is important to check the code each year and make sure it reflects the reality of your personal allowances as problems can occur. This is especially the case if you have changed jobs during the year, came from abroad or left the country during the year, earned very little or on an irregular basis, or if you reached retirement during the year. The **tax year** runs from 6 April to 5 April the following year.

You might find that you are due a rebate for overpaying tax. HMRC does send out letters to those whose income is low if it thinks they are paying tax when they should not be. But you cannot rely on HMRC to pick up every case of overpayment.

 The tax code tells your employer how much Income Tax to deduct from your pay packet and is covered on pages 26-33.

# SELF-ASSESSMENT TAX RETURN

Around nine million people each year complete a self-assessment tax return. For some, this is a way of declaring additional income to HMRC. For others, it is a once-a-year alternative to PAYE. Despite its name, self-assessment does not mean that you necessarily have to work out the fine detail of your taxes. HMRC can calculate the amount due from the figures you provide as long as you send them back soon enough. It guarantees to do this if you file your paper return by 31 October following the end of the tax year. You can also work out your own tax bill or employ an accountant to do this for you. If you file

 Failing to complete a form that you are sent, failing to tell HMRC that you have a new taxable source of income, or sending in your form after the 31 January deadline can attract automatic penalties and interest payments. Criminal sanctions are available for severe breaches of Income Tax law (see pages 195-6).

**" Despite its name, the self-assessment payment can be calculated for you by HMRC. "**

13

online, the HMRC (or other compatible software) will work out the amounts owing for you. So you only need HMRC to do the calculations if you file using a paper return.

The main categories of people who need to fill in a self-assessment form include the following:

- **The self-employed.** See pages 60–2 to see if you fit this category, but don't forget that this can include untaxed earnings from spare time work, money you make from a hobby, or your earnings from car boot sales or internet auction sites.
- **Employed people with perks,** such as a company car, accommodation from their employer, or a work-based private healthcare scheme where the tax hasn't been collected through the correct PAYE notice of coding.
- **Anyone whose earnings take them into the higher 40 per cent or new 50 per cent tax bands** if they have any savings interest or dividends from stocks and shares.
- **Those with capital gains** to declare (see page 20).
- **Anyone who was sent a form,** even if they have no income at all to declare for the tax year in question.
- **Individuals in receipt of rental income** from land and property in the UK.

If you are in any doubt, send in a form. You cannot be fined or otherwise penalised if you declare everything on time, even if it turns out that you do not owe any further tax.

**❝ If you are in any doubt, send in a form. You cannot be fined or penalised if you declare everything on time. ❞**

## AVOIDANCE OR EVASION – WHAT ARE THE BOUNDARIES?

**Avoidance** is reducing your taxes to the minimum using methods the tax inspector (or the courts) have held to be legal. **Evasion** is everything else from the deliberate under (or non-) reporting of income to claiming a computer for business use that is only used by your children for game-playing.

Tax-avoiders hark back to a 1936 legal case known as 'Inland Revenue Commissioners and Duke of Westminster'. This concluded: 'Every man (women hardly ever paid tax in 1936 – married women especially had no rights) is entitled to order his affairs so the tax attaching under the appropriate act is less than it otherwise would be.' This could be interpreted as you can take advantage of everything going unless it has been specifically banned.

But over the years, HMRC has chipped away at this judgement. A landmark 1981 legal case ('Ramsey and Commissioners of Inland Revenue') said the Inland Revenue (as HMRC then was) could clamp down on artificial schemes designed specifically to avoid paying taxes – the test is whether your affairs would have been arranged in this way had there been no tax to consider. This allowed tax inspectors to probe beneath the surface of certain complicated transactions.

HMRC can now demand that new tax avoidance schemes be registered with it as soon as a client is provided with information about a scheme so it can test their legality, should it wish. Importantly, there is no guarantee that a scheme which is legal now will still be approved in the future – a fact discovered by some people who had bought expensive Inheritance Tax avoidance schemes only to find later on that the law had changed after they purchased the plan but before they died, necessitating starting all over again.

Much evasion, however, is less sophisticated, such as the black economy where people work for cash and never declare their existence to the tax authorities. HMRC spends a substantial amount of time and effort in checking that traders who advertise in sweet shop windows or local newspapers are registered for tax.

## NATIONAL INSURANCE

National Insurance is the most important revenue raiser after Income Tax in the amount it brings in each year to the Treasury. Everyone pays it who is aged between 16 and state retirement age with earnings from employment or self-employment, unless they are very low. But if you carry on working after the state retirement age (see box, overleaf), you no longer pay National Insurance.

**For more information on National insurance: see pages 52-8 if you are in employment or page 77 if you are self-employed.**

You only pay it on your earnings from employment or self-employment. It is not payable on pensions, investment income, interest from savings accounts or money you make from letting out property. Most National Insurance is deducted from salary cheques or wage packets by employers using the PAYE system.

Despite its name, National Insurance now has little to do with health or unemployment insurance although some state benefits depend on your paying a set number of minimum contributions over a period of time – in some circumstances you could make 'voluntary contributions' (see page 56).

In most ways, then, National Insurance is simply another tax on earnings from employment or self-employment. This is shown most clearly with the National Insurance surcharge – a 1 per cent levy on all applicable earnings over the standard National Insurance upper-limit level – currently £43,888. This gives no state benefits whatsoever.

 National Insurance is calculated weekly on earnings from employment. You can pay National Insurance on earnings if they exceed the weekly minimum (£110), even if you do not earn enough in a year to pay Income Tax.

## State retirement age

This is currently 65 for a man but for a woman it rises, starting April 6th, 2010, on a month-by-month basis from 60 to 65 for those born between 6 April 1950 and 5 April 1955. For example, Emmeline was born on 10 May 1951 – 13 months after the start of the changeover period. So she will qualify for her State Pension when she is 61 years and one month. Josephine was born on 21 March 1955, so she will qualify for her State Pension when she is 64 years and 11 months old. Zadie, however, was born on 6 April 1955 – she will have to wait until she is 65 years old – as will all women born after her. By 2046, the state retirement age is planned to rise to 68 for both women and men.

**❝ National Insurance now has little to do with health or unemployment insurance, although some state benefits depend on you contributing. ❞**

# Taxes on spending

There are a number of taxes on spending. These are usually added automatically to the cost of goods and services that you buy. Understanding how and where they are levied, however, can help you choose between one way of spending your money and another.

## VALUE ADDED TAX (VAT)

Who does this apply to? Traders with a turnover (income from sales) in excess of £70,000 must register and collect any VAT due, irrespective of their own profit level.

VAT is a sales tax on a wide variety of goods and services, which is effectively paid by the end consumer. It is payable all the way along the 'production line', however, so as a raw material is turned into a finished item and then moved from factory to wholesaler to retailer, VAT is paid and then reclaimed by each of these traders along the chain.

Currently, VAT is paid at a standard rate of 17.5 per cent on a wide range of goods and services providing the supplier of the goods and services is VAT-registered. The following items are zero-rated: fresh food; train and bus tickets; air tickets; books, newspapers and magazines, and children's clothes. Domestic power supplies and contraceptives, among other things, are taxed at 5 per cent, and postage and health services are exempt from VAT.

Adverts aimed at consumers must show VAT-inclusive prices. Those in trade publications intended for businesses can print VAT-exclusive prices. It is not the consumer's responsibility whether the trader is liable to register for VAT or not. You can always ask the trader for a VAT number (and check it with HMRC) if you think a non-VAT trader is asking for the tax. Traders cannot come back to you later and demand VAT if they did not charge it at the time of the invoice. It is immaterial whether you pay in cash or in another way.

## Shifting boundaries

The boundaries between zero and the full rate can be confusing. Smaller adults can often fit children's VAT-free clothes and footwear – helpful for items that cross the age divide, such as sporting wear. Whether an item is taxable or not can lead to long drawn-out court cases. Cakes are VAT-free, biscuits are not. So where does a Jaffa Cake fit? After many years of disputation, the Jaffa Cake was declared to be a tax-free food. Chocolate chip cookies are zero-rated, but if the same amount of chocolate were to be spread on the outside of a biscuit, it would then have to be taxed at the standard rate.

A trader with an annual turnover below the VAT-registration limit has the choice whether to register or not. Some will legitimately not register so they can offer clients lower charges. Others will find it advantageous to sign up for VAT (see pages 78–82).

## INSURANCE PREMIUM TAX

Insurance Premium Tax is a tax on general insurance premiums, including household cover, pet insurance and motor insurance. There are two Insurance Premium Tax rates.

A standard rate of 5 per cent, which is charged on most policies. A higher rate of 17.5 per cent for travel insurance and some insurance for vehicles and domestic/electrical appliances – mostly extended warranty contracts, motor breakdown schemes and other forms of maintenance contracts.

Insurance Premium Tax is included in the premium you pay. Some insurers like to separate it out but this is only to show the 'real' price you are paying. You cannot reclaim or avoid paying this tax. Most long-term insurance (such as life or

---

### Ask the expert

#### What about VAT on second-hand goods?

If your business has dealings in second-hand goods, such as cars, antiques, collectibles or any other pre-used items, the way you charge VAT is determined by the second-hand scheme, formally known as the VAT margin scheme.

Normally, VAT is charged on the value added at each stage of the process that takes goods or services from first stage of production to final consumer. For instance, a car would go through many stages from raw materials to parts to assembly to retailer to final purchaser. At each of these stages, VAT is added to

reflect the increasing value of the vehicle. With second-hand items, this does not apply. The only added value is the profit made, so VAT is only charged on the profit margin – what the customer pays less what the goods cost to buy in from their original owners.

For most second-hand traders, this will be the entire amount they make each quarter before the expenses of running the business. In general, traders are not expected to show the VAT element to customers as this would reveal the mark-up they make.

---

To find out more about what excise duties are payable and at what rates, go to the HMRC website: www.hmrc.gov.uk and click on the 'Excise & Other' link in the Businesses & corporations box at the top of the home page.

critical illness or income protection) is exempt from the tax. There is no VAT on insurance policies.

# EXCISE DUTIES

These are taxes on the production (or importation) of goods such as petrol, tobacco and alcohol rather than on the value of their sales. There is a wide variety of rates – they can be found on the HMRC website (see box, below). Excise duties are included in the price of

the goods, so any VAT is then added to the duty paid value.

Excise duties are worked on the weight or volume of the goods – not their actual value. So the excise duty on a 70cl bottle of 'vin ever-so-ordinaire' is the same as on a bottle of premier cru. On the former, it is a large percentage; on the latter, it is barely noticeable. There are different rates for different types of alcohol, while pipe tobacco is rated lower than cigarettes.

## Ask the expert

### How much can I bring in from overseas without paying tax or duty?

When travelling from a non-EU country (including the Canary Islands, the Channel Islands and Gibraltar) you can bring in up to £390 of goods, such as souvenirs or clothing, into the UK for your own use without paying UK tax or duty. It is the value of the goods when they arrive that counts rather than what you paid for them. So, if you exceed this level, you must pay Customs duty and VAT on the full value of the item or items that take you over the threshold. In addition, anyone over 17 can bring back goods including up to 200 cigarettes, four litres of table wine, 16 litres of beer and one litre of spirits.

Goods obtained in the European Union (EU) (this does not include the Channel Islands or the Canaries) will already include the VAT and duty applicable to the country where the goods were obtained. Even if this is different to the

UK's tax rules, you do not pay any more (except for goods from some eastern European EU member states, including Bulgaria and Romania).

The goods must be for your own use and not for resale, even for payment-in-kind, such as a swap of the goods for services. You can generally bring back up to 3,200 cigarettes, 10 litres of spirits, 90 litres of wine and 110 litres of beer from the EU.

Anyone bringing back larger amounts can be questioned by Customs officers and asked for an explanation. While 200 litres of beer or wine could be for a big celebration, a car full of rolling tobacco would not be for personal use – tobacco has a short shelf life and no one could smoke that much. Customs officers can confiscate the goods and the vehicle as well, although this has been the subject of a number of legal challenges.

# Capital and investment taxes

These are taxes to pay when you buy certain assets, such as shares, and when you sell or dispose of certain assets profitably. There can also be additional taxes to pay on the estate someone leaves when they die. But providing you do nothing (or stay alive), there are generally no taxes to pay and no forms to fill in.

## CAPITAL GAINS TAX (CGT)

**Who does this apply to?** Largely to those who sell assets they own, including shares, investment properties, second homes and valuable works of art.

Known as CGT, it is paid on the increase in value of any possessions or investments you sell (or in certain circumstances give away or swap) between the time you acquired the asset and the time it is sold. Some items are exempt – the most important of which is your only or main home.

Working out any CGT bill is really easy. It is just 18 per cent of the profits you make when you sell – except for a few business owners who could pay less.

There is, however, an annual CGT exemption or free slice. It changes each year in the budget but it is now £10,100 (2010–11). If your chargeable gains in a year do not exceed the annual exempt amount, no CGT will be payable. This amount applies whether you use it or not and remains the same whether your gains are small or enormous. But you cannot carry unused relief over from year to year. It's use it or lose it.

You can, however, offset certain losses against your gains. So, if you dispose of one shareholding that has decreased in value since you acquired it by £10,000 and another that is calculated to have made £10,000, the loss is offset against the gain and there will be no tax to pay. For more information on CGT, see pages 134–42.

## STAMP DUTY

**Who does this apply to?** Anyone buying shares, unit trusts or investment trusts.

Stamp duty is levied at 0.5 per cent of the purchase price of most share purchases including investment trusts. Packaged products such as unit trusts or pension schemes or insurance-based investments do not charge the percentage explicitly but as they have

*“ There is an annual Capital Gains Tax (CGT) exemption or free slice, which changes each year. ”*

to pay it on each purchase, it is built into the cost of the plan.

You cannot reclaim this. But some investments such as bonds including government bonds (gilts), shares bought at flotation (also known as Initial Public Offerings (IPOs)), and investments based on shares but where you do not actually own the underlying investment such as contracts for difference, spread bets, futures and derivatives do not attract stamp duty.

## INHERITANCE TAX (IHT)

**Who does this apply to?** The tax is on the estate people leave when they die and may also apply to some transfers of value (gifts) made during an individual's lifetime, for example, transfers of more than the nil-rate allowance (£325,000 in 2010–11), into a trust. However, as it is possible to use certain exemptions and other planning devices to reduce the tax, it is of importance to everyone. It is levied at 40 per cent on death transfers and 20 per cent on lifetime transfers.

IHT is payable on your estate after you die. It counts the value of everything you leave (whether there is a will or you die intestate), including assets that you have either already paid tax upon or which were income and/or CGT free (such as the value of your main residence, or certain investments such as Individual

Savings Accounts or National Savings Certificates). It also includes the value of relevant transfers of value you have made in the seven-year period ending with your death.

There are two rates on death: zero and 40 per cent. Provided the total value of your estate and gifts made in the last seven years is under £325,000 (2010–11), your estate will pay no tax after you die. Anything over and above this level is charged at 40 per cent. It is paid out of your estate to HMRC by your executors – in practice, by the lawyer or other person who obtains probate.

There are a number of ways to reduce the value of your estate, and these are covered in Chapter 8. Alternatively, you could, of course, decide to 'grow old disgracefully' – spending some or all of your money on riotous living and having a good time. This is also known as 'SKI-ing' – Spending the Kids' Inheritance.

**❝ To reduce the value of your estate you could always spend some or all of your money having a good time. ❞**

For more information on working out your potential IHT bill and ways of potentially reducing your IHT bill, see pages 144 and 147-60. For dealing with probate, see the *Which? Essential Guide* to *Wills and Probate*.

# Taxes on property

The main property specific taxes are Stamp Duty Land Tax, paid on the vast majority of home purchases, and Council Tax, which is paid by everyone to their local authority.

In addition, second or investment homes can be subject to CGT when you sell – and all your property goes into the calculation for IHT.

## STAMP DUTY LAND TAX (SDLT)

This tax applies to anyone buying a residential property worth more than £125,000. This is increased to £250,000 for first-time buyers. It also applies to all non-residential land purchases over £150,000. SDLT is paid on purchasing most homes – only a minority are now in the exempt zone.

There are four rates – 0, 1, 3 and 4 per cent – and the rate you pay on the whole transaction value is the percentage that applies to the final pound. You pay 4 per cent on properties worth over £500,000 so you would have to pay 4 per cent on top of the entire purchase if your new home changed hands at £500,001 but only 3 per cent if it was exactly £500,000. SDLT cannot be reclaimed unless you have been overcharged in error.

## COUNCIL TAX

All householders, whether they are renting or buying or have outright ownership have to pay Countil Tax. Some landlords will add this tax into the rent so it is not paid directly.

Council Tax is an annual charge (still called domestic rates in Northern Ireland), based on how much your home is worth. This is not the current value but the amount that would have changed hands in April 1991 although this should have been adjusted if there were any substantial changes to the property (such as a large extension or a sub-division into flats or vice versa). It is paid to the local authority, which sends out Council Tax bills each year in April. It does not appear on your tax return. There are two ways in which a Council Tax bill can be reduced: second adult rebate and Council Tax Benefit (see page 175).

 See pages 174-5 for a breakdown of the SDLT rates together with information about 'disadvantaged' areas.

# Giving money to good causes

If you are a taxpayer and make gifts to charity, you might be able to claim tax relief on your donation and so increase the amount the charity receives.

Giving £100 to a charity without using Gift Aid gives the good cause £100. But if you use one of the following methods, the same money can be worth £128 in the hands of the charity. And if you are a higher or additional rate (40 or 50 per cent) taxpayer, your donation could give you a higher-rate tax relief. You could also boost your generosity by giving away assets such as shares or property or by leaving money to charity in your will. Here are some ways to achieve this.

## GIFT AID
By making a Gift Aid declaration you can allow a charity to which you donate to reclaim basic-rate tax from HMRC on your gift. This now applies to any amount given to any registered UK charity whether national, international or local (and certain other good causes), but not foreign charities unless they have registered in the UK.

Charities will send you a Gift Aid declaration or you can download it from the HMRC website (see box, below). For small amounts in cash or cheque, a simple declaration on an envelope or even an acknowledgement on a sponsorship form (where there is a clear name and address) is usually enough.

But for Gift Aid to work, you have to be paying enough Income Tax to cover the amount the charity will reclaim. So if you give £100, you must have at least £125 of taxable income per year – the charity reclaims the extra £3 to make £128 under a special arrangement with HMRC designed to last until April 2011.

Higher-rate taxpayers can claim back the difference between the basic and higher rate of Income Tax on any gift aid donations. They can do this through their self-assessment annual return. On £100, this amounts to a further

 Non-taxpayers should not use Gift Aid as they will create a tax liability for the charity which, in theory at least, they could find themselves being asked to pay.

 The HMRC website is www.hmrc.gov.uk. For more details about Gift Aid declaration, see helpsheet IR342. For further details on giving to charity, including information for higher-rate taxpayers, see the leaflet IR65, 'Giving to charity by Individuals'.

£41.66. There is no legal obligation to forward this extra tax relief to the charity in question or any other.

## GIFTS OF INVESTMENTS AND LAND

By giving away shares, stocks or securities or property to a charity you can claim a deduction from your taxable income on the market value at the time of the donation plus any costs, such as stockbrokers' fees. There is the added advantage that these transactions are also free of CGT. Similar tax relief is available for gifts of land or buildings. Donors have to show that the charity has accepted the gift to get the tax relief. See the HMRC leaflet IR178 'Giving Land, Buildings, Shares and Securities to Charity for Further Details'.

## PAYROLL GIVING

This is similar to Gift Aid in its effect on the charity, but involves less effort by the donor provided their employer runs a payroll-giving scheme. Here you agree to make regular donations to charity through deductions from your salary or wage packet. The tax relief is given automatically. Donations are subsequently deducted from your gross pay (before PAYE is applied).

Payroll giving attracts tax relief at your highest tax rate. This means that it costs you £8 to make a £10 donation (the charity can reclaim a further 21p under a special arrangement with HMRC) if you are a basic-rate taxpayer, and only £6 if you are a higher-rate taxpayer. There is no legal obligation on an employer to offer this scheme.

**"Payroll giving is similar to Gift Aid in its effect on the charity, but it involves less effort by the donor."**

# Working for an employer

When you work as an employee, your Income Tax affairs should be simple. Everything due ought to leave your salary via Pay As You Earn (PAYE). But there are a number of ways in which you can help yourself to tax savings. This chapter looks at these, guiding you through the tangle of tax codes and the mysteries of National Insurance deductions.

# Pay As You Earn

Pay As You Earn (PAYE) is the cornerstone of the UK tax system. Invented towards the end of the Second World War, it is designed to deduct the correct Income Tax and National Insurance from employed people – including company directors.

PAYE ensures that around two-thirds of the taxable population need never see a tax form. But the system is not foolproof. Each year there are mistakes. The most likely error scenarios are when you start your first job, when you change employer, return from a period of not working and when you retire.

## THE MYSTERIES OF PAYE

The PAYE system applies primarily to your income from employment but the same system is used for taxing most company and private pensions (but not the State Pension). Under PAYE, the employer (or pension provider) takes tax directly out of your wages, salary, stipend or pension – all these variations are known in tax-speak as 'emoluments'.

The system works around a tax code – a letter and number – which each employee or relevant pensioner is given on an annual basis. Your employer then consults HMRC tax tables to find out how much Income Tax and National Insurance (where relevant) to deduct.

In most cases, those responsible for payroll work use electronic tax tables. But whether it is online or on paper, the table together with your tax code should take any tax allowances (including the Personal Allowance) and tax deductions (a company car, for example) into account to come up with the right tax payment, which is then sent directly to HMRC.

Every year, your employer has to send you form P60 at the end of the tax year. This shows how much you have earned during the year and paid in Income Tax and National Insurance. This may be accompanied by form P11D, if you have taxable perks, such as a company car or health insurance. For a few low-paid employees, form P11D is replaced by form P9D.

At whatever point you leave a job during the tax year – whether for

**“ At the end of each tax year, your employer has to send you form P60. It shows how much you have earned in the year and paid in Income Tax. ”**

## Ask the expert

### How does the tax code work?

Your tax code is normally made of letters and numbers, and is usually shown on the payslip accompanying your pay or pension. The number tells you how much tax-free pay you're allowed in each tax year. This is divided by 10 – decimals are ignored. So if your allowance is limited to the Personal Allowance – £6,475 in 2010–11 – the number will be 647.

The letter gives your employer further information on the type of allowances you receive (see page 32 for a description of what each letter means).

Your tax code may go beyond just your salary. It can also be used to collect tax on fringe benefits – taxable perks, such as a company car or private medical insurance scheme for example – or to deal with income from other sources that are taxable but where no tax has been deducted (such as the State Pension or amounts under £2,000 due from a self-assessment form).

These amounts are deducted from your allowances, and give you the tax-free pay you are allowed in the tax year.

As a simple example, if your Personal Allowance is £5,000 and you have no other allowances or deductions, your number will be 500. The same person who acquires a taxable company perk worth £1,000 would have a 400 number.

But if the person with the 500 code had overpaid the previous year through an error by the tax on £500-worth of benefits, the number part of the code would go up to 550, so there would then be a greater slice of tax-free pay each month.

another job, retirement or unemployment – your employer must give you a P45. This shows how much you have earned and how much tax you have paid in the tax year to date.

## Allowances that can be set against tax

Allowances and reliefs increase your tax-free pay. If you are eligible for any of the following allowances or reliefs, check they have been included in your coding notice. See Income Tax allowances on page 29 for current allowance figures.

• Personal Allowance (given to every taxpayer resident in the UK, see page 10), or the increased Personal Allowance if aged over 65 years at any time during the year of assessment (not given to higher earners).
• Blind Person's Allowance.
• Married Couple's Allowance – also given to those in civil partnerships but

now limited to those where one partner was born before 5 April 1935.

- A deduction for work expenses or essential professional subscriptions or registrations – these will generally be agreed beforehand with the tax inspector. The work expenses are generally around health and safety issues while the professional subscriptions must be to an organisation where membership is compulsory if you are to carry out your job.
- Higher-rate (40 per cent) tax relief on payments into a personal or stakeholder pension through a company sponsored scheme. Payments that are made into pension plans elsewhere are dealt with through the self-assessment form. This relief will be reduced graduating to 20 per cent for those earning £150,000 or more for the 2011–12 tax year under present plans.
- Tax-relief for higher-rate taxpayers on Gift Aid donations to charity – this is through a company deduction scheme usually known as Give As You Earn. Your employer will tell you if there is a scheme and if there isn't, a number of charities will be more than happy to help your employer set one up! You receive higher-rate tax relief on other charitable contributions that you

**Tax tip**

If you receive a new allowance – perhaps you have reached 65 or become registered as a blind person, tell HMRC so that your code can be recalculated. Equally, if you receive a new taxable perk, check that your code changes otherwise you may have to find a large lump sum later.

make directly to the charity concerned, via the self-assessment form.

## Deductions on which you have to pay tax

Deductions effectively reduce your allowances so that you get less tax-free pay. Items that you have to pay tax on include the following:

- Most fringe benefits from your job, such as private medical insurance or a company car.
- Earnings not taxed under PAYE, such as some commission income and tips. Some trades operate a fixed deduction amount for tips, which may be greater or lesser than the actual amount received. If you do an extra one-off freelance job for the employer, then the code should be adjusted. You can also ask HMRC to adjust your code if you have a relatively small amount of self-employment (especially if it is regular) – this way you pay it on a weekly or monthly basis rather than in a lump sum at the end of the tax year.

- Taxable state pensions and benefits.
- Student loan repayments.
- Taxable rental income – most will pay this separately through their self-assessment.
- Taxable savings income with no tax taken off or, for higher-rate taxpayers, an adjustment for higher-rate tax owed on savings income – but only if you opt for this and it, along with other adjustments, comes to a tax bill of no more than £2,000. Otherwise it will be payable through the self-assessment mechanism.
- Underpaid tax. Where you have underpaid tax via PAYE this will usually be collected by adjusting your tax code in a future year. For example, tax that was underpaid in 2009–10 will usually be recovered through the 2010–11 tax code.

## WHAT YOUR EMPLOYER HAS TO DO

PAYE places a number of legal duties on employers. They are responsible for collecting the tax and National Insurance and then paying it to HMRC. They will normally ensure that if there is a special tax allowance for your job – such as for protective clothing – that you receive it. Your employer will also adjust your tax code to take account of deductions to repay student loan company borrowings.

HMRC considers the amount an employee receives in their pay packet is the correct sum after all deductions. Unscrupulous employers occasionally tell casual and contract staff paid in cash who demand their legal right to full-time staff benefits that they will report them to HMRC for evading tax as illegal

| Income Tax allowances | |
|---|---|
| | 2010-11 |
| Personal Allowance | £6,475* |
| Personal Allowance for people aged 65-74 | £9,490 |
| Personal Allowance for people aged 75 and over | £9,640 |
| Married Couple's Allowances aged 75 and over | £6,965 |
| Minimum amount of Married Couple's Allowance | £2,670 |
| Blind Person's Allowance | £1,890 |

*Progressively withdrawn at £100,000

 To find your local Citizens Advice Bureau (CAB), go to www.citizensadvice.org.uk. See also the information about The Taxpayers' Charter on pages 202-3.

self-employed workers if they push their claims. They cannot do this. If they did, the employer would be responsible for the tax and National Insurance on top of what they have already paid. It is the employer's job to check who should be on the payroll and an employee and who should be outside of it as a self-employed contractor.

Errors such as failing to deduct for a new taxable perk should be adjusted through the tax code – but you should always check on this. An accountant, trade union or Citizens Advice can help.

Employers who fail to pass on tax and National Insurance face penalties (including imprisonment) and interest charges. Employees are not liable to

pay tax again when employers take the money from pay packets and disappear (unless they are found to have an involvement in the failure to pay).

## MORE THAN ONE CODE?

You get a separate tax code for each job or pension. Your Personal Allowances will be given against what you, or your tax office classes as your main job or pension, which is usually the one that pays the most.

This leaves you paying tax on second jobs without any allowances as you have used them up in the first job. Your pay will be then taxed at the basic rate (20 per cent), the higher rate (40 per cent) or the additional rate (50 per cent). If this results in you paying too much, or too little, tax over the year, an adjustment will be made at the end of the tax year and your tax code will probably change. Employers should know about this possibility via the letter in your tax code.

 If you suspect your or another employer of cheating by not deducting Income Tax or National Insurance properly, or by deducting it and then pocketing it, phone the Business Anti-Fraud helpline on 0800 788 887.

## " Employers who fail to pass on tax and National Insurance face penalties and interest charges. "

### Tax tip

You can ask your tax office to allocate your allowances differently. For example, if you have two part-time jobs, you can ask that your allowances be split between them both, rather than having them all set against your main source of income. This can be useful if the two income sources vary substantially month by month.

## WHEN DOES THE CODING NOTICE ARRIVE?

A coding notice that tells you how your tax code is worked out should normally arrive by the January or February of each year. This enables employers to put any changes into effect for the start of the new tax year.

But not all employees necessarily get a coding notice. For instance, if the letter in your code is L, P, V or Y – and this takes in the majority of people – your employer may be able to alter your code number automatically, to take account of the new allowances in the budget that year.

 If your employer does not know what your tax code is, you will be taxed on the emergency code of 647L in 2010-11 (the same as 2009-10). This gives you only the basic Personal Allowance for someone aged under 65. To get the correct tax code, give your employer your P45, if you have one.

## PEOPLE AGED 65 OR OVER

If you are 65 or over, you are eligible for an increased Personal Allowance, which increases further if you are over 75. You will also be eligible for the Married Couple's Allowance if either you or your spouse (or civil partner) were born before April 1935. The full amount of the allowance or relief will appear on the right-hand side of your coding notice.

## CIRCUMSTANCE CHANGES

You must keep HMRC informed of any change in your circumstances, even if your tax affairs are normally dealt with through PAYE. Some examples are given to the right.

• **You get married,** enter a civil partnership or separate (only for older people for Income Tax allowance purposes but this can be important for savings income, capital gains, and IHT).

• **You start to receive a second income** (see page 35).

• **The amount of untaxed income** you receive increases or reduces (but unless this is substantial, this is done through the self-assessment form – HMRC does not want to know every time a small untaxed savings account changes).

• You have a change of address.

• If you are approaching the ages of **65 and 75.** HMRC needs also to know when women reach state retirement age (as this can vary due to the phasing in of female State Pension retirement ages) so National Insurance payments can stop.

 If you are aged over 65 years, see pages 10-11 for further information on age-related allowances.

# Tax code letters

Here is a description of what the tax code letters mean.

| | |
|---|---|
| **BR or DO** | All your pay from this source is taxed at the basic rate (BR) or higher rate (DO). This is because it is a second (or subsequent job) and you have used up all your allowances elsewhere. If you are on the BR code, you should check that your total earnings from employment are not over the top-rate threshold (currently £43,875). If so, you would be liable for the 40 per cent tax rate (see also OT). |
| **K** | Your total deductions exceed all your allowances. This occurs generally when the taxable value of fringe benefits or perks, such as a company car, company housing or medical scheme, are greater than your personal and other allowances. A 'K' code is effectively a negative number. |
| **L** | This is the most widespread coding. Here you get the basic Personal Allowance and no more. |
| **NT** | There is no tax due on this income – this generally happens when the earner is not resident in the UK for tax purposes. |
| **OT** | You have used up all your allowances elsewhere so there is no tax-free pay. Instead, you pay tax at the basic 20 per cent rate and then the top 40 per cent rate as applicable. |
| **P** | You get the full age-related Personal Allowance for someone aged 65–74. Used most commonly on pension payments. |
| **T** | Used if your tax office needs to review your tax code. You can also ask your tax office to use it if you don't want your employer to know your personal details, such as the fact that you have another job as well. It does not mean that you have been given a temporary tax code. |
| **V** | You get the full age-related Personal Allowance for someone aged 65 to 74, plus full Married Couple's Allowance for couples aged under 75, and you are likely to pay basic-rate tax. Mostly used in pension codings. |
| **Y** | You get the full age-related Personal Allowance for someone aged 75 or over. Mostly used in pensions. |

## WHAT TO DO IF SOMETHING IS WRONG

If you think your tax code is wrong, you need to tell your tax office as soon as possible to make sure you pay the right amount of tax. If it is wrong, you may be due a tax refund, or you may need to pay more tax. You can contact your tax office by:

- Looking on your coding notice for the address.
- Asking your employer for the tax office details.
- Asking your pension provider (if you receive a pension through PAYE).

If too much tax has been deducted, the overpayment will first be set against any other tax you owe. For the remainder, you should be sent a cheque, so long as the amount is over £10. If the amount is small or you are feeling generous, you can elect to have it sent to a charity where it will be boosted under the Gift Aid Scheme.

If you haven't paid enough tax, the outstanding amount will be collected by adjusting your tax code for a future tax year. You will be asked to make a repayment direct to HMRC if the amount is above £2,000 or if you no longer have income taxed under PAYE. If the amount is very large, you may be able to come to an individual agreement with the tax inspector over a repayment schedule. A specialist accountant should be able to help negotiate this.

> **“ If too much tax has been deducted, the overpayment will be set against any other tax you owe. If there is anything left over – and this is more than £10 – you will be sent a cheque. ”**

33

# When circumstances change

The PAYE system is designed to cope with most changes in your working life with adjustments made automatically as your earnings change or you move from job to job or from job to unemployment or vice versa.

At the following key points you need to be particularly alert and make sure that you have the right forms and that HMRC has the right information.

## STARTING WORK

When you first start work you will not have the P45 form from a previous employer. This could also apply if you have been out of the labour market for some time although if you were receiving a benefit such as **Income Support** or **Jobseeker's Allowance**, you should get a P45 form from the benefit payer. The P45 is the form you take from employer to employer to ensure PAYE continuity.

If you do not have a P45 form, your employer should give you a **P46 form** to complete. This will be sent to HMRC, which uses it to calculate your tax code.

Until you have a code, your employer will normally use an emergency tax code based on the standard Personal Allowance. But if you start work any time other than at the beginning of a new tax year the emergency code may cause you to pay too much tax because it cannot calculate the fact that you have not been earning until then. Your emergency tax code overpayment (if any) will be refunded as soon as the correct code is supplied.

## Jargon buster

**ES40 booklet** You get this when you wish to return to work after a long period away from paid employment

**Incapacity Benefit** A long-term sickness benefit

**Income Support** A means-tested benefit for those below State Pension age who are out of work or ill

**Jobseeker's Allowance** A non-means-tested benefit for those out of work but actively looking for a new job

**Statutory maternity, paternity or adoption pay** Money from the state when you are off work due to pregnancy and the birth of a child or the legal adoption of a child – it is only paid if you do not receive a minimum amount from an employer and it is taxable

**P46 form** A form that you take to a new employer if you have never worked before or have been out of the workforce during the whole of the tax year when you start the new job

**Statutory sick pay** Payment from the state when you are off work due to illness – it is only paid if your employer does not continue paying you. It is taxable

## PERIODS OF NON-WORK

A number of state benefits, such as statutory **sick pay** and statutory **maternity, paternity or adoption pay**, are taxable. So is any extra sick pay or maternity pay your employer gives you as part of your contract of employment.

Payments from private sick pay insurance schemes (such as income replacement plans and permanent health insurance policies) that you arranged and paid for yourself are tax free. But payments from a company scheme to cover periods of illness are taxable.

The state Maternity Allowance (this is paid to those ineligible for statutory maternity pay) is tax free. **Incapacity Benefit** is usually taxable after 28 weeks of payment with the tax deducted through PAYE.

## CHANGING JOBS

When you leave your job, you should be given a P45 form by your old employer. You need to hand this to your new employer, to ensure the correct amount of tax is deducted from your pay. The alternative is that you complete a new P46 form, as if you were starting work for the first time. This will generate an emergency code, which may need to be changed, depending on your circumstances. You could end up overpaying tax and having to wait to have this refunded. You may wish to use a P46 if you do not want your new employer to know what you earned in your last job.

## TAKING A SECOND OR SUBSEQUENT JOB

If you have a main job and a part-time job or several part-time jobs, one of these will normally be treated as your principal employment. As you will not be leaving a job when you take a second or subsequent employment, you will not get form P45. So you will have to fill in a P46 for each job. Provided you earn enough in your main job to use your allowances, subsequent jobs are generally taxed at the basic rate. You should have a BR tax code (see page 32).

But if your earnings elsewhere are such that you fall into the top tax band, your tax code should be DO (see also page 32). This avoids underpayment. You should also take care, however, to complete the P46 accurately as having several jobs often produces problems.

If you overpay, you can make a claim for a refund.

**❝If you have a main job and a part-time job or several part-time jobs, one of these will normally be treated as your principal employment.❞**

**35**

## LOSING YOUR JOB

If you are made redundant, walk out of your job or are sacked, you should be given a P45, which you need to take to your local Jobcentre Plus. Any unused tax-free entitlement is set against the taxable amount of any Jobseeker's Allowance you get. Means-tested Income Support is tax free. Any tax you have overpaid will be refunded at the end of the tax year (or when you stop claiming benefit if this comes sooner).

## RETURNING TO WORK

When you return to work after a period of unemployment covered by Jobseeker's Allowance or Income Support, you need to fill in the form from **booklet ES40**, supplied by Jobcentre Plus. Return this to the jobcentre, which will issue a form P45 for you to give your new employer.

## RETIRING

When you near retirement, you should inform your tax office in good time, as your tax code may need to be changed. However, if you are not yet 65 (whether a man or a woman) or you have high earnings, you will not qualify for the higher-age-related Personal Allowance. If you have a private or an occupational pension, or a mix of the two, your main pension provider should arrange for you to continue paying tax through PAYE.

As far as the Income Tax system is concerned, all that has happened is you have swapped employers. But once you stop work, you should no longer have to pay National Insurance.

**❝ If you are retired and have a private or an occupational pension, or a mix of the two, your main pension provider should arrange for you to continue paying tax through PAYE. ❞**

**Attempting to hide your earnings by having them paid to an offshore company counts as tax evasion and can be – and has been – punished with imprisonment plus confiscation of assets bought with the tax that was concealed.**

For more information about what happens to your tax in later years, see pages 100-116. See also the *Which? Essential Guide: Finance Your Retirement.*

## WORKING ABROAD

If you work abroad full-time, whether for a UK or a foreign employer, your foreign earnings will normally not be subject to UK tax providing that you work overseas for a complete tax year.

You are allowed to visit the UK for 91 days or less during any tax year and still keep your foreign residency benefits. You are also allowed to do some work during these 91 days and you can work for a UK company from your overseas base – even if the work concerns UK affairs.

If you work abroad but do not meet these criteria, your foreign earnings are taxable in the UK and must be declared. To avoid paying tax twice, it is possible to claim a reduction in your UK tax bill against any overseas tax paid. There are special rules for seafarers, which are operated by their employers.

### Defining a 'day'

In cases where it is unclear whether a person has actually properly moved abroad and changed their tax residence, HMRC has recently moved towards a stricter interpretation of what a 'day' constitutes. It previously regarded this as a complete midnight-to-midnight 24-hour period, so if you arrived at 1am on a Monday and left at 11pm on a Tuesday, neither of those days counted. Now it is counting the hours in these 'incomplete' days - an anti-avoidance measure designed to stop the very rich with private planes commuting between work here and their tax haven homes.

### Tax tip

You could 'tele-commute' via email and the internet while living in a sunnier or cheaper locality and not pay UK tax. You would, however, normally be liable to pay tax in the country in which you are living unless this is somewhere with a tax-free potential, such as the Channel Islands or Monaco. There are special benefits for authors in Ireland.

> ❝ Foreign earnings will normally not be subject to UK tax, providing that you work overseas for a complete tax year. ❞

 For more details see HMRC leaflet IR20 'Residents and non-residents: liability to tax in the UK'.

# Tax benefits at work

This section looks at what your employer can legitimately give you of value that does not count for Income Tax or National Insurance, which includes perks, expenses and other benefits.

Most of what you earn, including overtime, bonuses, commission, tips and holiday pay, counts towards your taxable income. However, there are some payments and benefits-in-kind from your employer that are tax free. These do not have to be declared if you are sent a tax return.

**"**Some benefits are tax free; no matter how much you earn, they don't have to be declared. **"**

## Tax tips

As an employee, you can save tax by:
- Making the most of tax-free fringe benefits, such as medical check-ups, free shares (see pages 44-5) and childcare vouchers.
- Claiming mileage allowance if you use your own vehicle or bicycle on company business.
- Maximising pension contributions.

## PERKS WHERE TAX IS NEVER CHARGED

Some benefits are tax free, no matter how much you earn. These include:

- **Employer contributions** to your approved pension fund.
- **Subsidised staff canteen.** Facilities can be split into blue collar and white collar or higher- and lower-paid staff providing the food is the same in each eating area. This can also include outside catering, such as a local restaurant, providing the general public cannot eat in the same room at the same time.
- **Luncheon vouchers,** but only up to 15p a day. This sum has remained unchanged for some 40 years (the equivalent of 15p bought a lunch in the 1960s). If the voucher is higher, you still get the first 15p tax free.
- **Workplace nurseries.** These must be exclusively for employees of the organisation or shared with other employers. They do not have to be physically at the workplace. Otherwise,

 See pages 100-16 in the chapter on pensions and retirement for information concerning pension contributions.

there is a £55-a-week limit on tax-free vouchers or similar paid over to an approved childcarer or nursery.

- **Pool cars.** These must be kept overnight at the place of work and be available for more than one employee. Any private use must be incidental. But emergency service workers are exempt if they have to take their pool vehicles home in an emergency or when on call.
- Disabled person's travelling expenses.
- **Education.** A number of courses are tax free.
- **Long-service awards.** The minimum time is 20 years and it can't exceed £50 for each year of employment.
- **Awards under company suggestion schemes,** but these are barred for those whose normal job is to think up ideas. The award must be 'commercial' (related to its value to the company) and must not exceed £5,000.

## Tax tip

Your employer can give you a Christmas, summer or other party tax free providing the spending per head does not top £150 including VAT. This annual sum can cover more than one occasion. But if the spending tops £150, the whole amount (and not just the balance over £150) is taxable as a fringe benefit.

- **Mobile phone bills,** when the phone is given by the employer.
- **Redundancy counselling.** Services such as help with CVs, outplacement advice and training on interview skills.

## TAX-FREE EXPENSES

There are a number of expenses that your employer might give you to perform your tasks better, which do not change the amount of tax and National Insurance you pay. These include:

- **Reimbursed expenses** for which your employer has a formal agreement with HMRC, known as a **dispensation,** so that they can be ignored. Ask your employer if in doubt.
- **Reimbursed expenses** where your employer makes a **voluntary agreement** with HMRC to pay the tax on the perk on your behalf – this might include business dining where you, as the employee, have the benefit of a free meal while entertaining customers or contacts.

## Green tax tips

'Green' tax-free perks include:
- Sports and similar recreational facilities, but not membership of a commercial gym where facilities are available to the public.
- 'Green commuting'. Free or subsidised work bus travel, bicycling facilities including workplace parking, safety equipment and showers (see Getting a bike for around half price, pages 40-1).

*Continued on page 42*

**39**

# Green tax tip: Getting a bike for around half price

There are a number of little-known tax benefits designed to encourage bicycle use to travel to your workplace and use at your workplace.

✓ There are tax- and National Insurance-free initiatives such as the provision by employers of bike sheds and showers; and the 20p-a-mile tax-free allowance if you use your bike for work travel (for visits to other sites, meetings, and so forth but not commuting).

✓ One total oddity is the 'cyclists' breakfast' – a firm can provide cyclists with a free breakfast on up to six occasions a year, which is tax free as well. HMRC does not dictate the menu!

✓ But the biggest potential saving is via the Green Transport Plan. This effectively means you can have a new bike (pedal or electric) for as little as half the price others would pay. What happens is that employers set up a scheme with a local bike shop, a bike shop chain, or one of the special schemes that allow you to buy your new two-wheeler at the shop of your choice (most cycle retailers are in one plan or another).

✓ You choose your bike (plus accessories that you can justify on safety grounds, such as a helmet, lights, locks, carrier rack) and the employer pays the bill to the shop or to the scheme. Your boss then leases the bike to you, deducting the cost from your salary – usually over 12 months. But as the money comes from the very top of your wages slip, it is deducted before it reaches the Income Tax and National Insurance stage. In addition, employers who are VAT-registered (the majority) can deduct the VAT on the bike purchase against their own tax. At the end of the lease period, the employer 'sells' the bike to you for a pre-agreed nominal sum.

✓ A £300-bike package under this scheme becomes £255.32 after VAT at 17.5 per cent. Divide that by 12 and each monthly payment is £21.28.

✓ The 'salary sacrifice' is before tax and National Insurance – for a basic-rate taxpayer this payment is equal to around £15 a month in after tax income. The total cost over the year, therefore, is £180. Factoring in free interest (comparing with a typical credit card) brings it down to around around £150, or half the original price. If VAT rises, payments fall.

✓ For the higher-rate taxpayer, the saving is greater – it's £12.83 a month or £153.91 over the year (and that's before the interest-free loan boost).

✓ There is no limit on the value of the bike in tax law. And bike shops say many people using the scheme end up buying a bike worth twice what they would otherwise have paid. But employers can set a limit to the bike's purchase price if they wish. The paperwork is generally carried out by the bike shop or the scheme, leaving the employer to finance the leasing.

There are three potential disadvantages:

✗ You cannot use the scheme and claim the 20p-a-mile cycling allowance (you can, of course, once you own the bike outright).

✗ You are supposed to use the bike for commuting to work – but no one expects you to do this when the weather's bad or if it is too far (using the bike to reach a local station would count).

✗ Reducing your salary with a sacrifice (where you give up part of your top-line earnings to improve your overall take-home pay by using the tax system in your favour), can affect your mortgage borrowing capacity and your pension entitlements.

- **Mileage allowance payments** (to agreed limits) if you use your own vehicle for work (but not travelling to and from work). The maximum is 40p per mile for the first 10,000 miles and 25p per mile thereafter. Motorcycle usage can attract up to 24p a mile and there is a 20p-a-mile allowance for work use of a bike. Where employers pay less or nothing, the employee can claim the difference against personal tax.
- **Payments of up to £2 per week for extra household costs** if you regularly work at home by arrangement with your employer. Your employer may pay more if you are able to supply evidence that this covers reasonable extra household costs.
- **Late-night taxi travel,** when this is to ensure employee safety. However, this tax-free expense cannot be offered to someone whose regular work time includes unsociable hours.
- **Accommodation,** but only when this is necessary for the job (such as a school caretaker) or where this is 'customary' (such as some agricultural work) or where there is a specific threat to the employee's security (such as members of the armed forces).

- **Medical check-ups,** including eye tests for health and safety reasons.
- **Parking** at or near the workplace either paid for or provided free of charge by your employer.

## TAX-FREE LUMP SUMS

Extra payments, such as bonuses, from your employer are generally treated as salary and taxed as usual. But some payments are tax free. These include:

- **Most lump sums** from a registered employer's pension scheme.
- **The first £30,000 of most redundancy payments** or compensation paid by your employer if your contract is broken.
- **Compensation for an injury** or disability that means you are unable to continue with your job.
- **Gratuities** on leaving the armed forces.

# TAX-DEDUCTIBLE EXPENSES

If a reimbursed expense is *not* covered by a dispensation, you are still able to claim a deduction for expenses you incurred 'wholly, exclusively and necessarily' in the course of your work. The most important of these three words is 'necessarily'. This can be tough to prove – it cannot be for something where spending makes your work easier or more effective. These might include:

- **Business travel,** but this does not include travel to and from work in the normal way. This can be complicated – you may get tax-free travel if you have to travel to a work location that is not your normal one or with 'triangular travel' (where you travel from your home to a location that is not your normal workplace before going to your normal workplace and then home again).
- **Reasonable hotel and meal expenses** associated with business travel – the emphasis is on 'reasonable'.
- **Protective clothing and uniform** necessary for your job, and other work-related items for which flat rate allowances are available.
- **Heating, lighting and telephone costs** if you are compelled to work at home (but this is very restricted).

- **Relocation costs** if you have to move home for your job – up to £8,000 per move. This is intended to cover removal costs including expenses involved with selling a property you would not otherwise have sold and buying a new one. Companies can offer more – some will do so and pay the additional tax charge for you.
- **The cost of a visit by your spouse** or civil partner and any minor children you have if you are obliged to work abroad for a continuous period of 60 days or more – this is limited to two trips a year.
- **Death benefits** paid to your dependants.

> **❝** If a reimbursed expense is not covered by a dispensation, you are still able to claim a deduction for expenses you incurred 'wholly, exclusively and necessarily' in the course of your work. **❞**

 For more information about when business travel is a tax-deductible expense, see the HMRC guide EIM31800 'Tax relief for business travel', and for protective clothing and uniform, see the leaflet 'Expenses and benefits in kind'.

## TAXABLE FRINGE BENEFITS

These include benefits that are taxable for those earning over £8,500 a year including the value of the benefits and those that are always taxable, irrespective of earnings.

## Benefits taxable for all but the lowest paid

In contrast to the tax-free benefits listed overleaf, the following 'perks' normally add to your tax bill, unless you earn less than £8,500 a year (including the value of the perks), when they are tax free. This £8,500 has been unchanged for three decades – originally those earning over £8,500 a year were called 'higher paid'. Now the £8,500 is less than the national minimum wage for a full-time employee.

If you are to be taxed on the benefits, they will be listed on form P11D given to you by your employer once a year. If you qualify for the under £8,500 concession, your perks will be noted on form P9D instead. But there is still a big advantage to the employee of a benefit-in-kind. There is no National Insurance charge on such extras. For the basic-rate taxpayer, a perk instead of salary will generally reduce the total government deduction from 31 per cent (20 per cent tax and 11 per cent National Insurance) to 20 per cent. These include:

- **Free fuel**, taxed at the same rate as your company car on a notional value (see also box on page 46).
- **Private medical insurance.** This is taxed at the cost to the employer

## Green tax tip

Company cars are taxed at 15–35 per cent of the car's list price according to the car's carbon dioxide emissions (see box, page 46), including the cost of delivery, accessories and VAT.

and is usually considerably less than you could buy equivalent cover on an individual basis.

- **Loans of goods,** taxed at 20 per cent of their value, or the annual rent if that is higher.
- **Loans of money.** Above £5,000 (see interest-free loans on page 42), any interest saved because you are charged less than the HMRC official borrowing rate is taxed as income.

## Benefits taxable for all, irrespective of income

You always pay tax on these benefits – even if your income is low. The cost of the benefit is added to your other income. This is to prevent employers paying very low wages and then making it up with fringe benefits and perks.

- **Company credit cards.** These are taxed on the cost of purchases unless these are work-related and tax deductible.
- **Accommodation.** Free or subsidised housing is taxed as a benefit unless it is integral to your job. You are taxed on the annual rent or gross rateable value of the property less any rent you pay. If the property costs your employer more than £75,000, you must pay

additional tax, unless you are already being taxed on the full open market rent for such a property. In addition to this, unless you are earning less than £8,500 a year (including perks), you pay tax on loans of furniture and other expenses that have been met by your employer, such as heating your home.

- **Vouchers and tickets.** These are treated as additional income for tax purposes unless they are vouchers for benefits that are tax free, such as eye tests.
- **Shares and share options** that are received outside an 'approved scheme' (see pages 49–51) are treated as income for both tax and National Insurance purposes.

## COMPANY CAR – YES OR NO?

The company car was once the best perk around. It offered big tax savings – and it told the world (especially your fellow employees and your neighbours) that you had arrived work-wise. Whether it is still a status symbol is debatable as the company car has lost much of its tax break allure.

The number of company cars on the road has fallen by around a quarter since the start of this decade. That said, for some drivers, not having to worry about spending and time-consuming items, such as insurance and maintenance, may outweigh any tax or cost benefits or dis-benefits – where you lose out financially but gain perhaps from a hassle-free existence.

## Swap the car for extra salary?

Today, many company car owners 'trade in' their car and take a salary increase instead (which can help with mortgage applications and pension contributions as well), or they opt for other car ownership routes. You might be better off buying your own car in the normal way. You might, for example, be happy with an older or smaller car or decide you can live without one altogether, hiring a car when you really need one.

> **"The company car was once the best perk around. Whether it is still a status symbol is debatable as it has lost its tax-break allure."**

### Tax tip

If you own your car or are buying through a scheme that you (and not the employer) are responsible for, you can charge the company a tax-free 40p a mile for the first 10,000 miles of business use. You can even claim an extra 5p a mile for each work-related passenger you carry – so it could be 60p a mile in a full five-seater car. After 10,000 miles, it is down to 25p a mile, but you can still claim the extra for a passenger.

## " If you receive extra salary in place of a company car, it will be liable for tax. "

If you opt not to have a company car but to receive extra salary instead, this money is liable for tax and National Insurance together with the rest of your pay.

In working out the best option, you need to consider several factors, including the type of car your employer might provide, the amount of business miles you drive each year and the cash equivalent your employer is prepared to offer. A comparison site, such as www.cashorcar.co.uk, might be useful if you find it difficult to decide. Your employer or a benefits consultant may also be able to help.

There are a number of car financing schemes that offer the advantages of the company car without Income Tax implications. You could purchase a vehicle through a leasing scheme that gives the advantages of a company car (not having to worry about repairs, etc.), but without any potential tax complications. This is often known as the 'virtual' or 'clone' company car.

Before committing to any course of action, obtain comparative pricings of the company car, using a specialist financing scheme versus running your own car and claiming tax-free mileage allowances. You can get this information from specialist accountants, benefits consultants or car companies. Also factor in any expected salary increases, especially if they would take you into the top tax band.

### Green tax tip

The company car as a taxable perk used to be charged on its engine size. This was changed in 2002 so there are few company cars still remaining under this scheme.

Now it all depends on a combination of its CO2 emissions and its original purchase price – usually the list price for the car plus any accessories, but not including anything used to help drivers or passengers with disabilities. You now pay tax at between 15 and 35 per cent on its list price, depending on its official CO2 emissions rating.

From 2008, company cars with an emissions rating of 120g/km or less of CO2 have been taxed at a lower rate of 10 per cent of the list price. This may influence your choice of vehicle.

 For more information on CO2 emissions, contact the Vehicle Certification Agency at www.vcacarfueldata.org.uk. This website also gives you a list of eligible models (petrol and diesel) with low emissions: go to 'Useful information' and click on the 'How to use the data tables' tab.

# Car-related tax-free benefits

If you have to opt for a company car, the following items from your employer (continued overleaf) can be provided without any tax or National Insurance complications:

- Maintenance and repairs
- Servicing
- Motor insurance
- Road tax
- Membership of a motoring organisation or membership of a road rescue scheme

## Case Study — Claudia

Claudia starts her new job at £40,000 a year. She is offered a Jeep Cherokee company car worth £22,340 or £3,000-a-year extra salary to fund her own purchase. She drives 15,000 miles a year of which 4,000 are business miles. The car is expensive, has a high 246 emission, and her business mileage is low. But she is still around £53 a month better off with the company car option than the personal contract 'clone'. Here, the cash alternative is not attractive. She could, however, go back to her employer and suggest upping the £3,000 to £4,000 when the two figures would balance. If she had received a yearly £5,000 as an alternative, she would be better off turning down the company car.

# Vehicle excise duty 2010–11

Cars registered on or after 1 March 2001 will fall into 13 categories for the annual road tax (vehicle excise duty) depending on their $CO_2$ emissions. In addition, there is a special first year rate for larger cars. The www.vcacarfueldata.org.uk/ has details of the category in which your car/intended car purchase fits.

| Band | $CO_2$ (g/km) | Standard rate | First year rate |
|------|---------------|---------------|-----------------|
| A | up to 100 | £0 | £0 |
| B | 101–110 | £20 | £0 |
| C | 111–120 | £30 | £0 |
| D | 121–130 | £90 | £0 |
| E | 131–140 | £110 | £110 |
| F | 141–150 | £125 | £125 |
| G | 151–165 | £155 | £155 |
| H | 166–175 | £180 | £250 |
| I | 176–185 | £200 | £300 |
| J | 186–200 | £235 | £425 |
| K[1] | 201–225 | £245 | £550 |
| L | 226–255 | £425 | £750 |
| M | over 255 | £435 | £950 |

[1] Includes all cars over 225 $CO_2$ registered between 1 March 2001 and 23 March 2006.

For cars registered before March 2001, the cost of the tax disc is based on cubic capacity of the engine:
- Under 1,500cc:   £125
- 1,500 cc and over:  £205

You cannot count travelling to and from your normal workplace to your home as company car mileage.

- London (or similar) congestion charges (if your employer pays these for you and you are on company business)
- Parking fees on company business
- Depreciation
- Finance charges.

## Private fuel mileage

The same percentage as on the car itself – 15–35 per cent, but the lower 10 per cent rate (see the green tax tip on page 46) is used to work out the taxable benefit you pay on fuel that you receive for private mileage.

This figure is calculated on a notional sum of £16,900 rather than the cost of fuel you actually use and, using the car's tax percentage, gives an annual tax bill of between £3,380 and £6,760.

## PAYE checklist

Ensure you have verified all the following items that are applicable to you to make the most of tax-favoured deals and to prevent errors in your tax bill.

- Check the tax code on your payslip (see pages 26–33).
- Claim for tax-deductible expenses (see page 43).
- Make sure you get a P60 each year (see page 26).
- Take up any tax-free fringe benefits that your employer provides – ask your employer to provide others, such as the bike scheme (see pages 40–1).
- Declare perks that are taxed on your self-assessment form (see pages 44–5).
- Work out the pros and cons of having a company car (see pages 45–8).

# Investing in your workplace

An increasing number of companies offer employees shares under various schemes so they can gain from the firm's success. However, stocks can fall as well as rise and you could suffer along with investors if the stock price falls.

## Company employees only

This section only applies to employees in companies – if you work for a partnership, charity, a not-for-profit company, the Government, a local authority, the NHS or a trust, then this is not for you.

Many share schemes have tax and National Insurance benefits and are known as approved schemes. These include plans such as Save As You Earn (SAYE), Share Incentive Plan (SIP), Company Share Option Plan (CSOP) or Enterprise Management Incentives (EMI).

SAYE is the most widespread scheme. The Share Incentive Plan is also used by a number of companies but most of the other schemes and those that are taxable – known as unapproved schemes – tend to be mainly used by small companies or as complex methods of executive remuneration.

## SAVE AS YOU EARN

This is offered by a large number of public companies including many in the FTSE 100 index – although there is no obligation on any employer to have a scheme or on an employee to join.

SAYE is the most popular because it combines tax benefits with a 'can't lose' guarantee. If your company's shares rise over the life of the SAYE contract, you can profit. But if they fall, you can walk away from the deal with some interest on your money.

The plan has to be open to all employees, irrespective of status, salary or whether they are full or part-time. But companies can impose a qualification period of up to five years' service.

> **❝SAYE combines tax benefits with a 'can't lose' guarantee. ❞**

### SAYE: a savings contract for a fixed period

If you join, you contract to pay in a monthly sum from £5 to £250 into the plan. You agree to pay for three or five years – those that opt for five years can leave the money for a further two years, making seven years, although it is up to the company to say which time periods will be allowed. You cannot increase your payment once you start.

When the plan starts, the company will announce the value of each share for the SAYE. This can be set anywhere between the stock market value on that day and 20 per cent below that.

Many companies start a new scheme each year so you could add to your original payment, providing your total does not top £250 a month. If you decrease your payment into the scheme, it counts as stopping, which ends the scheme for you. You can, however, miss up to six payments during the contract period, which then extends the length of your contract.

The money you save goes into a special bank or building society account selected by your company. This cash grows with tax-free interest followed by a tax-free bonus at the end of the period. During the saving contract you do not buy shares and the interest rates vary from time to time. If you stop within the first year, there is no interest, while if you stop short of your contracted time, the interest rate is very low.

Your contract ends if you leave the company – but you can continue if leaving the firm is due to illness, retirement, or redundancy. If you die, your family can take over your contract.

## What you do when your contract matures

At the end of the contract, you compare the price of the shares with the starting price. If it has gone up, you turn the savings into shares (which you can sell whenever you want). The gain in the share price is not taxable as income. If it has fallen, you just walk away from the deal, taking your cash plus the tax-free interest.

 **If you sell the shares, you will be liable for CGT on the gap between what you receive for them and the price you contracted to pay for them, which is known as the option price. But provided this profit is less than the annual CGT exemption (see page 20), you will pay no tax.**

## SHARE INCENTIVE PLAN

With a share incentive plan, the risks are greater. You actually acquire the shares, unlike SAYE where you have a contract to purchase them in the future from which you can walk away if it does not work out. So you will have to live with the ups and downs of share values.

Shares can be given free by your employer or you may have to pay for some. But even if you buy them yourself,

*" The money you save in SAYE goes into a savings account selected by your company where it grows tax free. "*

they come from money that is free from Income Tax and National Insurance and there is no CGT charge if shares are sold immediately after removal from a plan. However, you don't actually own the shares when you acquire them. Instead, they are held by trustees in a special plan for three to five years, depending on the specifics of each scheme.

## Free shares

Employers can put up to £3,000-worth in any tax year into the trust scheme on your behalf. They must be available to all employees, including part-timers, but there can be a qualification period of up to 18 months. Free shares can be given in line with performance targets, length of service or salary level.

## Partnership shares

These are shares you buy with your own untaxed money. You are limited to £1,500 (or 10 per cent of your gross salary less pension and charitable contributions if that is lower). Because of the tax and National Insurance freedom, a £1,500 purchase is worth a discount of almost £500 for basic-rate payers and nearly £615 for higher-rate payers – the £1,500 paid as a salary to a basic-rate payer would end up at around £1,000. You have to hold the shares in the trust for five years to keep the tax benefits.

## Matching shares

Companies can (but don't have to) give up to two free shares for each partnership share that you buy. This is an alternative to free shares. So you could get up to £3,000 in tax-free benefits.

## Share dividends

Dividends are taxable when they are paid in cash. But if the dividends are re-invested in the scheme (up to a £1,500-a-year limit), then the money is not taxed. This can continue as long as you hold shares within the plan.

## NON-APPROVED SCHEMES

With non-approved schemes, the value of the shares you receive is taxed as additional income. Where you pay a reduced sum for the shares, you are taxed on the difference between this and their market value. This charge applies to other investments like loan stock, bonds, unit trusts and futures. Non-approved schemes are mainly used to incentivise and remunerate key employees in small companies.

**If you are not sure a scheme is approved, ask your employer.**

Information on these schemes can be found in HMRC helpsheet IR287 'Employee share and security schemes and capital gains tax' and online at www.hmrc.gov.uk/shareschemes.

# National Insurance

When it first started six decades ago, National Insurance was charged at a fixed rate per week and provided a menu of benefits closely linked to payments or 'stamps'. Now it is a tax in all but official name; some forms of National Insurance pay the same benefits no matter whether you pay at the minimum level or the maximum, and other classes of National Insurance offer no benefits whatsoever.

## A TAX ON EARNINGS

National Insurance is a tax on earnings from your job and on any profits you make from self-employment. It is not levied on other forms of income you may have, such as savings account interest, dividends on shares, or rental income, nor is it charged on capital gains.

How much you have to pay depends on whether you are employed or self-employed and how much you earn. You stop paying it once you reach State Pension retirement age (see box, right), irrespective of whether you continue to work or whether you take the State Pension or defer it until later.

By paying National Insurance you qualify for certain state benefits, such as the basic State Pension, Incapacity Benefit and, in many cases, the Jobseeker's Allowance paid to those out of work. All these benefits are non-means tested and they are known as contributory benefits. Means-tested benefits, such as the Pension Credit or Income Support, do not depend on a National Insurance record – they are non-contributory benefits.

## How you pay it

Those in employment pay through regular deductions via Pay As You Earn (see pages 26–33). Those in self-employment can pay annually – some of it may be via their self-assessment return (see page 182).

### Tax tip

You should stop paying National Insurance when you reach state retirement age – 65 for a man and 60 (rising from 2010 to 2015 from 60 to 65 (see page 16)) for a woman on earnings from employment. If you are an employee, you will need to give your employer form CA4140/CF384 'Certificate of Age Exception', available from HMRC National Insurance Contributions Office (for details, see page 213). You will need to repeat this form filling exercise with any subsequent employers.

# Checking your record

Your contributions are recorded individually. When you are 16, whether or not you start to work, you are given a unique National Insurance number consisting of two letters, six numbers and a final letter (from A to D). You need this number for any enquiry about your record – call the helpline on 0845 302 1479 for further details of how you can acquire your personal data.

This payments record is used to calculate any contributions-based benefits entitlement. If you miss making National Insurance payments and don't receive credits (see below), this creates gaps in your record and reduces the amount of benefit you might receive.

## NATIONAL INSURANCE CREDITS

National Insurance credits are Class 1 contributions (see page 55) that you cannot pay because you are not working or not earning enough to come up to the lower earnings level. In general, National Insurance credits help you maintain your record for the State Pension, but they don't help you to qualify for benefits such as Jobseeker's Allowance.

Credits are added to your contribution record when you are:

- **Aged 16 to 19** and in full-time education (less any weeks where you did work earning at least the lower earnings level). The lower earnings level is £97 a week for 2010–11.

- **Out of work and signing on** with the jobcentre.
- **Incapable of work** through illness based on a medical certificate.
- **Attending some educational and training courses** when you are over 19.
- **Receiving statutory maternity pay or statutory adoption pay.**
- **On jury service** (if your employer stops paying you).
- **A full-time carer** (this can include looking after your children, see home responsibilities protection, overleaf).
- **A man aged 60–65 who is not paying contributions on earnings** – generally those who took early retirement.
- **Grandparents** who look after children aged up to 12 for at least 20 hours a week.

> ❝ National Insurance credits are Class 1 contributions that you can't pay because you are either not working or not earning enough. They help maintain your record. ❞

Credits are not paid automatically unless HMRC knows about your circumstances – for example, you must be signing on with the jobcentre or have a medical certificate. For some types of credits, you also have to apply in writing. The rules about when you get credits and when you have to apply for them can be complicated. If you have a query about National Insurance credits, you should consult the Citizens Advice Bureau (for website details, see foot of box, overleaf).

## Home responsibilities protection

Home responsibilities protection is a form of National Insurance credit that helps parents and carers to satisfy the contribution conditions for long-term benefits, such as the basic State Pension. It does not give you any more National Insurance contributions, but it reduces the number of years you would have to have paid contributions in order to get the full amount of benefit. This helps you if you are not working because you are bringing up a child or caring for someone.

You get home responsibilities protection for each year in which you get Child Benefit for a child under 16, or get Income Support because you are caring for a disabled person. While the home responsibilities protection is recorded automatically, this form of National Insurance credit can be very complicated and depends on individual circumstances. Ask the tax office if you are unsure – and then check any negative answer with Citizens Advice (see box, below).

*Continued on page 58*

> **" Home responsibilites protection can be very complicated – ask the tax office or Citizens Advice Bureau for advice if you need it. "**

---

### Case Study   Samantha

Samantha can't work because she has to look after her disabled son. She wants to ensure she has built up her basic State Pension for her retirement.

If she's married, she might be able to piggyback on her husband's National Insurance. But her more independent course is to apply either for Carer's Allowance, which will automatically give National Insurance contribution credits to allow her a full pension, or if she does not qualify for Carer's Allowance, to apply for home responsibilities protection (see above).

Home responsibilities protection would reduce the number of years Samantha would need to have paid contributions to get the full amount of pension. She will get this irrespective of her son's condition while she still has an under 16 dependant living at home. Once he is older, she can apply to HMRC for protection if she has to spend at least 35 hours a week looking after her son. It is not automatic.

---

 To find your local Citizens Advice Bureau (CAB), go to www.citizensadvice.org.uk. For more about Carer's Allowance, go to www.direct.gov.uk.

# National Insurance payments and entitlement

There are four main categories of National Insurance contribution (NIC), which are also known as 'classes'.

## Class 1 (employed)

You pay Class 1 contributions if you are an employee and under State Pension age. These are deducted by your employer, who also makes a contribution on your behalf based on your earnings – this employer contribution does not earn you any benefits. How much you pay depends on how much you earn.

- If you are below the lower earnings threshold (£5,720 or £110 a week for 2010–11), you pay no contributions but will build up the right to benefits, provided you earn above the lower earnings limit of £5,044 or £97 a week (2010–11).
- If you earn above the earnings threshold, you pay 11 per cent of your salary (gross earnings less £5,715) to the upper earnings limit of £43,875 (2010–11).
- On any earnings above the upper earnings limit, you pay a further 1 per cent – the so-called National Insurance surcharge. This buys no benefits.

If you have more than one job, with different employers, each one will deduct NICs if your gross pay from that job is above the lower earnings threshold. If your combined income from both jobs exceeds the upper earnings limit, there is a risk that you might end up paying too much (because although the combined total exceeds the limit, the separate incomes may not). To avoid this, you can ask to defer paying contributions on your second job until the end of the tax year, when your total income liability is calculated accurately. The same principle applies if you are employed in a job but also self-employed. In these circumstances, you can put off making Class 2 or Class 4 contributions.

Class 1 contributions (apart from married women's reduced rate, see the benefits box on page 57) give entitlement to:

- Basic State Pension
- State Second Pension – S2P (unless you are contracted out into an employer or insurance based scheme)
- Contribution-based Jobseeker's Allowance
- Short-term Incapacity Benefit
- Bereavement benefits.

Earnings subject to Class 1 liability also form the basis of your entitlement to statutory sick pay and statutory maternity, paternity and adoption pay. Only S2P payments depend on how much you pay in National Insurance on your earnings.

## Class 2 (self-employed)

You pay Class 2 contributions at the rate of £2.40 per week if you are self-employed and your profits are likely to be above £5,075. If you earn below this, you can opt not to pay National Insurance at all, but you won't build up any benefit entitlement. You can arrange to pay it via a direct debit or as one single annual payment. If your profits are above £5,715, you'll have to pay Class 4 contributions as well. If you work abroad and don't pay Class 1 contributions, you can often pay Class 3 contributions voluntarily to protect your contribution record.

Class 2 contributions give entitlement to:

- Basic State Pension
- Incapacity Benefit
- Bereavement benefits.

## Class 3 (voluntary)

Voluntary contributions are made by those who face gaps in their contributions record because they are either not working – and getting no National Insurance credits (see page 53) – or are exempt from paying Class 1 or Class 2 NICs , or live abroad. They are also paid by anyone (except certain married women and widows – see the benefits box, opposite) who wants to top-up their total contributions. The 2010–11 rate is £12.05 a week. Paying Class 3 contributions can often be worthwhile to ensure your benefit record is maintained if you are not working.

Class 3 give entitlement to:

- Basic State Pension
- Bereavement benefits.

**❝Class 2 National Insurance contributions are payable if you are self-employed and with profits in excess of £5,075.❞**

## Class 4 (self-employed)

You must pay Class 4 contributions (in addition to Class 2) if you are self-employed and make taxable profits above £5,715. The rate is 8 per cent on profits above £5,715 to £43,875. Additional profits above £43,875 attract a surcharge of 1 per cent.

There are no additional benefits above those already given by Class 2 contributions.

## Benefits

Not all contributions qualify you for benefits – the Class 1 married women's reduced rate payments offer very little. Class 4 gives you nothing while Class 1 on earnings above the lower earnings level offer nothing either other than higher State Second Pension.

## Tax tip

You could save tax if you can mix employment with self-employment. Someone earning around £20,000 a year from employment would pay about £1,650 in Class 1 National Insurance. But if they earn some £15,000 from employment and about £5,000 from self-employment, they would pay around £1,100 in Class 1 and just under £110 a year in Class 2 payments – a saving of nearly £400.

## In the 2011–12 tax year

All National Insurance rates will increase by 1 per cent.

- The standard employed person's rate will be 12 per cent, while the surcharge on higher incomes will be 2 per cent.
- The Class 4 rate paid by self-employed people will go up to 9 per cent.
- Employers will also see amounts they pay rising by 1 per cent.
- Likewise, those with incomes over £150,000 will also see the tax relief they receive on pension contributions cut to 20 per cent.

## CONTRIBUTORY BENEFITS

Although some state benefits (such as Income Support) are non-contributory, others are only available to those who have paid, or been credited with, a qualifying level of NICs. The amount you can claim might vary, depending on how much you have paid and on what class of contributions you have made – see box at foot of page.

### Tax tips

- Request a State Pension forecast to check your position. The Department for Work and Pensions will supply this (tel: 0845 300 0168) or write to the Future Pension Centre (see Useful addresses, page 212) and ask for a forecast application form (BR19) with a return envelope.
- Consider filling gaps in your contribution record, but be careful not to overpay. You should not pay any National Insurance other than the 1 per cent surcharge on earnings over £43,875 in 2010-11. Don't forget there could be changes in 2010. These will centre on reducing the number of years needed for a full pension payment to 30 years (see page 102).
- Know what benefits you are entitled to claim.

**❝ Make sure you request a State Pension forecast to check how much will be in your pension pot. ❞**

 For more information on contributory benefits, contact your local Jobcentre Plus (www.jobcentreplus.gov.uk), the Pension Service (www.thepensionservice.gov.uk) or the Department for Work and Pensions (www.dwp.gov.uk).

# Working for yourself

More than four million people are self-employed –
and that number is growing. They range from top
City lawyers earning a million or more to part-time
online traders making some extra pocket money.
This chapter tells you all you need to know to take
best advantage of the rules – and avoid running
foul of HMRC.

# Are you working for yourself?

Self-employed people can claim expenses and allowances to reduce their tax bill that are not available to those HMRC considers to be employed. Before you start, you need to know which side of the fence you fall.

## ARE YOU EMPLOYED OR SELF-EMPLOYED?

As well as being your own boss and working the hours you decide to do rather than having to clock on from nine to five, there can be substantial tax advantages in being self-employed. These can often be so attractive and save so much tax that many people who are really employed sometimes claim they are self-employed.

Increasingly, many people are both employed and self-employed in the same tax year so they fall into both camps.

 HMRC is devoting substantial additional resources to catching people who have failed to register their self-employment and dodge paying taxes and National Insurance (where applicable). HMRC employees scour adverts offering services in local newspapers and in newsagent windows to check if the advertisers are registered with it. They also collect notes pushed through doors promoting services such as cleaning and gardening as well as targeting online auction sites and car boot sales.

### Case Study  Natasha

Natasha is a university lecturer in geography with a full-time salary. But she also writes articles using her expertise for travel magazines and advises television companies on exotic locations for reality shows. Her salary from the university counts as employment, but her earnings from both the magazine writing and the television consultancy count as self-employment. If she had another source of income – turning her pottery hobby into a business, for example – she would have another, and separate, source of self-employment.

But there is also a growing number of people who may not even realise that they are self-employed. These include the increasing army of online traders and those who regularly take pitches at car boot sales.

## You are self-employed when ...

HMRC has a number of tests to ensure your status is correct. To claim self-employed status – and gain the tax advantages that can come with it – you have to be able to answer yes to the following questions.

- **Do you risk your own money in the venture?** Does the financial buck stop with you? If it goes wrong, you should personally lose out either by ending up working for nothing or suffering a money loss if you are genuinely self-employed.
- **Can you hire someone to do some work** for you as an employee or engage extra help at your own expense and when you want? This does not mean you have to hire people – merely that you can if you want.
- **Do you provide the main tools of your trade** (and not just small things such as a pen or a screwdriver)? You have to provide large items such as vans or computers as well as smaller items. You can, of course, either build the cost into your customer invoices or bill customers directly for certain throwaway items.
- **Can you decide when, where, and how you work?** The essence of self-employment is that you can work as much or as little as you wish.

- **Do you have to correct work** that proves unsatisfactory in your own time at your own expense?
- **Do you regularly work for a number of different people?** This is a key decider – someone who can answer yes to the first questions but who does not work for several clients would generally be counted as employed.

## You are employed when ...

You have to work set hours, are paid by time (hour, week, month, year), even if they might receive a bonus for overtime or extra work, can be moved from job to job by someone else, cannot employ extra help from their own pocket, and can be told what to do. The employed status includes those who are directors of their own companies. Employees are also those who are claiming work-related benefits such as Jobseeker's Allowance. You may have a number of employers – but as long as each one can tell you what to do and pays you for your time and supplies premises and tools, then you are employed.

**❝** You are employed when you have to work set hours, are paid by time, can be moved from job to job and can be told what to do. **❞**

 The HMRC website – hmrc.gov.uk – has a whole area devoted to self-employed taxation matters. It covers such things as registering as being self-employed and/or for VAT, filing the self-assessment tax return and making payments.

## If it's not clear ...

HMRC realises that there are always 'grey areas' where someone is genuinely not sure on which side of the line they fall. One frequent 'grey area' is where someone does spare-time work, such as delivering a lecture but on such an occasional basis that the source of earnings may not be repeated for some time or even some years. In practice, as long as you declare this one-off payment and pay all the tax due on it, you have a valid reason not to register as a self-employed person.

Your local Tax Enquiry Centre will give you a written opinion on whether you should register as a self-employed person or not, which you can appeal against should you wish.

### Tax tip

A small earnings exemption certificate is issued by the National Insurance Contributions Office to self-employed people with profits or anticipated profits below the level at which Class 2 National Insurance Contributions become payable. If you think this might apply to you, see form CF10, which can be found at www.hmrc.gov.uk/forms/cf10.pdf.

## YOUR FIRST DEALINGS WITH HMRC

When you are an employee, it is your employer's responsibility to ensure the correct tax and National Insurance amounts are taken from your salary cheque. But once you become self-employed, it is your responsibility to account for tax and, where applicable, National Insurance payments.

If you work for yourself, you will normally need to fill in the self-employment supplement to the self-assessment form (called SA103) as well as the main annual tax return, including any other sections, such as employment. If your self-employment earnings are relatively small (with total sales of no more than £15,000 a year) and you have no other complications in your tax life, you may qualify for the short tax return (see page 183).

Whether full- or part-time, you must tell HMRC when you start your business by calling the helpline for newly self-employed on 0845 915 4515. In return you will receive a number of leaflets to read and forms to fill in. If you fail to register within three months of becoming self-employed, you may have to pay a £100 penalty. The starting date is when you have realistically set up a business to provide goods or services – not the date on which you start to collect money from customers or move into making a profit.

 To get hold of form SA103, go to www.hmrc.gov.uk and click on the self-employed link in the 'Individuals and employees' box at the top of the home page. Alternatively, contact the HMRC orderline on 0845 9000 404.

If you do not register and evade tax, you will be liable for further penalties beyond the £100, including possible imprisonment.

## What about partners?

Partners in a business have to fill in different forms and are subject to some different rules. But what you can claim against tax from partnership earnings is broadly similar to the deductions that self-employed people – known as 'sole traders' – can make.

If you are in partnership with others, you need the partnership 'supplementary form' (SA800), as well as the main form but only one form needs to be filled in per partnership. It tells you that you must divide up the partnership profits in line with how each partner has earned that money. From there on, each partner is responsible for filing their own individual tax form with their share of the earnings from the partnership.

If you run your own company, even as a director or major shareholder, you are an employee of your business and need the employment self-assessment pages that are contained in self-assessment form SA101.

## Although two forms are required for a partnership, only one needs to be filled in.

## Case Study Andrew and Zara

Andrew and Zara are partners in their fashion design business agreeing to split the profits 40/60 (because Zara puts in more time and deals with higher paying customers). The SA800 return will therefore show that Andrew has earned 40 per cent of the partnership profits and Zara the balance of 60 per cent.

They have already set this down in a legal document known as a 'formal deed of partnership'.

# Expenses you can and cannot claim

Not all business expenses are tax-deductible. Here are some of the key expenses you can claim and some you cannot.

## Salaries and wages

You can include:

✓ The wages, National Insurance and other costs of anyone you employ. This could include pension provision, childcare costs, and life and/or sickness insurance policies.

✓ You can also claim for any costs in hiring another self-employed person to do specific work for you (but be careful they do not turn into an employee when you will be liable for employer's National Insurance).

You can't include:

✗ Your own wages or National Insurance (or those of a business partner if it is a partnership).

## Premises

You can include:

✓ Dedicated business premises: heating, lighting, cleaning, water rates, rent, business rates.

✓ If you are working from home, you can count a proportion of costs such as lighting, heating, cleaning and insurance, mortgage interest if part of the home used exclusively for business (but there may be CGT when you sell). Also add in the general maintenance of business premises (proportionally if working from home).

You can't include:

✗ The initial cost of buildings, alterations and improvements (but this may qualify for capital allowances, see page 67).

✗ The proportion of bills relating to the private use of your home.

## Eating out

You can include:

✓ A reasonable amount for subsistence when you have to be away from home and cannot use your normal facilities.

You can't include:

✗ The cost of entertaining actual or potential clients.

## Travel

You can include the following items if used wholly and exclusively:

✓ Fares on buses, trains, boats and planes.

✓ The running costs of a car or van – you can only apply for a part if the vehicle is also used privately.

✓ Hiring cars or vans.

✓ Parking charges.

✓ You can claim 20p a mile for travelling by bicycle.

✓ Travel and accommodation on business trips and between different places of work.

You can't include:

✗ Fines for parking and motoring offences.

✗ A claim for travel between your home and your workplace if that is different, but you can claim for travel from your workplace (even if that is your home) to where you have to carry out the work.

✗ The purchase of a car – that counts for capital allowances instead (see page 67).

## Administrative costs

You can include the following items if used wholly and exclusively:

✓ Insurance.

✓ Legal fees.

✓ Accountancy costs.

✓ Consultation expenses.

✓ Repairs and replacements.

## Other items you can include

✓ All those small things that make organising a business possible, such as phone and mobile phone expenses, postage, publications, stationery, fuel, gas, electricity, water.

✓ Advertising and publicity.

✓ Goods that you buy in for resale or that serve as raw materials for processing or manufacture.

✓ Bank charges and interest on a loan that is needed for your work.

✓ Pension contributions can be offset against up to 100 per cent of your self-employment profits (your turnover less your expenses) if you wish, provided the amount is within the overall limits (see pages 105-8).

## BUSINESS EXPENSES

The great advantage of self-employment (in part compensation for its uncertainty) is the ability to decide exactly how you will carry on your business – and that includes how you spend your money. What you buy in for your business – anything from computers to cardboard boxes – can be set off against your turnover (the amount that you take in from customers and clients of your goods and services).

When you are an employed person, expenses are very difficult to offset against tax. The test is very strict – the spending has to be 'wholly, exclusively and necessarily' incurred in carrying out your employment contract (see page 43). The emphasis is on the 'necessarily' so employed people can't claim tax against expenditure that makes their working life more pleasant or even more efficient. It is up to the employer to provide these items.

You may be able to claim for items that you use in your self-employment that you already owned before you started. For example, an online auction site trader could claim for the computer and the camera to take pictures of the goods on sale.

## The 'wholly and exclusively' but not 'necessarily' test

As a self-employed person, you are the boss and you can decide what is to be spent. Here the test regarding business expenses is 'wholly and exclusively' – note that the word 'necessarily' is no longer there. This gives you substantial freedom to run your business in the best way you consider possible.

The 'necessarily' has been dropped because no one else but you can decide what is necessary.

- Is it necessary to place a large or small advert for your services? No one knows.
- Is it necessary to buy something new or second-hand? Again, that's a commercial decision for your business – whether you get it right or wrong is your responsibility.

Within your spending capacity, you have the same spending choices as a major corporate concern.

---

### Tax tip

If you claim part of your home, make sure you list the space as 'non-exclusive'. This means it can be used for non-business use in the future. Don't claim mortgage interest or Council Tax on this as it could invalidate the CGT exemption on your main residence (see box, opposite). You might also run into business rate problems.

---

 Keeping on top of all your paperwork and up-to-date with tax law can be time consuming. See pages 182–96 for advice on dealing with your tax affairs and pages 204 if you think you could do with some outside help.

**If you can divide an expense between business and personal cost (car running costs, say, on the basis of mileage), the business proportion is deductible. If the nature of the expense means it can't be divided (such as an air fare that is for a journey that is part business and part pleasure) then no deduction is allowable.**

The wholly and exclusively still apply, however. Goods and services that you purchase must be for the business and not for your leisure time or for that of your family.

Anyone running a small business – especially a home-based business – may find the 'wholly and exclusively' tag difficult to apply to items such as computers, cars, telephones and premises. The normal compromise is to claim a proportion of these expenses for your business. Remember that the tax inspector looks first and foremost at how much you claim for business costs as a percentage of your overall turnover before delving into each individual item. With statistics from four million or so self-employed businesses, HMRC has a very good idea of how expenses relate to turnover in any given line of work.

Under the 'wholly and exclusively' label, you could perhaps justify a visit to Hollywood if you were in the film business but not if you were in the plumbing trade. Equally, a Rolls-Royce is reasonable if you run a wedding hire firm, but not if you're a plasterer.

## Claiming for capital allowances

All of the expenses listed on pages 64–5 are things that are effectively 'consumables' – once you have spent the money (on a phone call or a stamp, for instance) you no longer have the item. But other expenditure is on items with a longer shelf life, such as machinery and computers, which should serve your business from year to year until they are worn out or become obsolescent or inadequate for your purposes.

Here you claim 'capital allowances' – a proportion of the purchase cost of the machine that you set against your profits each year as long as you own the item so the tax relief on their cost is spread over a long time.

This process involves a first-year allowance – usually 30 per cent of the purchase price – and then 20 per cent of the declining balance each year.

Cars and vans have a set of special rules with limits on the value of the car that can be considered for this writing down. These rules exclude high value vehicles – currently £12,000 or over.

Allowances on capital items tend to change from year to year – often to incentivise certain purchases, such as energy saving products or computers.

## Short-life assets

If you dispose of an item for less than its written-down value (the amount it has reached after deducting each year's percentage), the balance normally continues to be written down gradually over future years (see case study, below).

But you can claim immediate relief for the balance if you have elected to have an item treated as a 'short-life asset' and you dispose of it within five years. This is useful for assets that wear out or date rapidly, such as computers. HMRC generally accepts computers in this category, but it is best to consult an accountant on less well-known items.

## KEEPING RECORDS

One of the biggest differences between employment and self-employment is that the self-employed have to keep records to show HMRC how much they have earned from the goods and services they supply and how much they have spent on items necessary to function as a business.

The basic advice is to keep a record of everything you buy and sell in your business. But beyond that, this includes items where you will be only able to claim part of the cost against tax, such as your home, if you use space at home as an office or workroom, or your car if you only use it partly for business. You must also keep records of what you have paid to anyone else, including members of your family.

## Case Study James

James buys a lathe for his woodturning business for £2,000. This comes within his annual investment allowance – currently £100,000. This allows him to deduct the cost of the machine against his tax bill. If he had already used his full £100,000 allowance, then he would be able to set off a percentage of the lathe's cost (depending on his firm's size). The remaining cost of the lathe would be set off against his tax bill in declining amounts each year.

For more information on cars with low carbon dioxide emissions, see www.eca.gov.uk or contact the Vehicle Certification Agency at www.vcacarfueldata.org.uk, who can also give you a list of eligible models.

You will need to do all this anyway to ensure that you know how well your business is doing and in order to pay the correct amount of tax.

However, you must also keep all relevant bank and building society statements together with all other financial paperwork, although you do not have to have a separate business account and there is no rule against dealing in cash.

Records do not need to be elaborate – simply sufficient to back up your claims for business expenses and to be able to prove your income.

However, HMRC does recognise that it is often difficult to account for all the small items that you can legitimately claim for. These might include bus fares, newspapers, and where you claim part of your heating and lighting bills for that home office/workshop, as it may often be impossible to split figures from your household bills accurately.

## Storing your records

As a self-employed person, you have to keep records for four years longer than for other self-assessment items. The rule is keep them for five years from the 31 January following the relevant tax year. So, for your 2010-11 return, you must keep them until 31 January 2017. You can be fined up to £3,000 if you don't, but this is normally only applied where there is suspicion of fraud. Once your self-assessment return has been accepted, you can lock up your records and you should never need to look at them again. But the long time slot gives HMRC a substantial window to revisit your accounts if it thinks you have underpaid.

## PRODUCING SELF-EMPLOYMENT ACCOUNTS

Preparing full accounts is both time consuming and costly – even those for a relatively small concern could cost £1,000 and require special paperwork. You may want to do this – and the expenses of the accountant employed for the audit is deductible from your profits – but most self-employed people do not need or require this effort and expense, nor does it generally provide any useful information to further the business. However, full accounts can have a

### Case Study  Ron

Ron sells a machine with a written-down value of £2,000 for £1,500 because he needs the money quickly and has a ready cash buyer. He can continue to claim the £500 difference against future tax years.

 If you think you are not keeping on top of your records sufficiently well, turn to pages 204-6 where there is advice on the different kinds of outside help that you can employ.

purpose if you wish to borrow money from a bank.

Under recently introduced rules, HMRC recognises three levels of self-employed business for self-assessment return purposes – the very small, the small and the rest. The key is turnover, which is the sales you make (and hence the money you take in) and not how much profit you make. So, a garden designer whose costs would typically be limited to travel and a small office would keep far more of what clients pay as profit than a gardener who has to buy materials, such as plants, out of customer payments.

## Very small businesses

If sales are under £30,000 a year, the category into which most part-time self-employed fall (as well as many working full time), then HMRC only requires you to fill in four figures on the tax return:

- The sales you make.
- The expenses you claim.
- Capital allowances (if any) (see page 67).
- The profit.

Use the form called 'self-employment (short)'. For your own purposes, it may help to create a fuller breakdown of your expenses – for instance, amounts spent on buying in plant and equipment or employing other people – but it is pointless submitting this as the tax system is simply not interested.

## Small businesses

For those whose turnover is over £29,999 but under £64,001, there is

a mid-way scheme where you can continue to fill in the short form. Here you still use the four headings – sales, expenses, capital allowances and profit – but you have to show each kind of expense. This should not need a professional and the payment of fees that goes with employing an outsider to finalise your figures, although many people do employ an accountant for this.

The expenses you need to show are:

- Wages (what you pay to others, including the self-employed).
- Travel.
- Costs of premises (such as rent and insurance).
- Advertising.
- Phone and internet.
- Costs of machinery and depreciation (the annual fall in the value of items you use in your business).
- Bank interest and other financial expenses.
- Accountancy fees.
- Bad debts (amounts your customers will never pay you).

## The rest

Once you go over £64,000, you must comply with the complete account disclosure on the full self-employment form. You may also have to send in a balance sheet. At this level, you will probably use an accountant, although costs can be reduced if you can supply the figures yourself rather than relying on a professional to calculate them from your books.

# Paying tax

You pay tax on profits from self-employment in two annual instalments via the self-assessment form. But besides needing to finance these payments, you also have to watch special rules that operate in the first and final years of your business. There may also be advantages (and sometimes drawbacks) in choosing an accounting year that does not coincide with the tax year.

## WHEN YOU ARE TAXED

Your profits are worked out for an accounting period, typically one year, and you can choose when your accounting year ends. Most self-employed people, especially if it is spare-time earnings, choose the tax year ending on 5 April as the easiest date as this fits in with their earnings from other sources, such as employment and investments. For convenience, HMRC now accepts that a 31 March year-end is equivalent to the real end of the tax year a few days later. This is known as a fiscal year end.

When you start a business with a fiscal year end, you have to pay tax on the first months up to the end of the tax year, even if that is less than 12 months. You may have to estimate your payments if you do not have accounts.

But you – or an accountant advising you – may wish to select another date. This can help you defer tax by giving you longer to file your self-assessment return and more time to keep your profits in the bank.

❝ Most self-employed people choose the tax year ending on 5 April as the easiest date as this fits in with their earnings from other sources, such as employment and investments. ❞

More information on how and when you pay your tax is given on pages 182-96 in Chapter 10, Dealing with your tax affairs.

## NON-FISCAL YEAR ACCOUNTING

Each tax year, you are taxed on profits for the accounting year ending during that tax year. For instance, if your accounting year ends on 30 April, in 2010–11 you are taxed on profits for the business year to 30 April 2010. And as you could pay the first part of that bill

### Tax tip

If your turnover (the amount of business you do) does not top £40,000 in a year, you can opt just to show your sales and expenses figures in presenting your profits. But you must still be able to show the tax inspector how you arrived at that figure if you are challenged. Where your total tax due under self-assessment is £2,000 or under, you can opt to pay this through your PAYE code (assuming you are employed or in receipt of a pension) (see pages 26–33) for the following year, spreading out the payments over the full 12 months. Although you don't have to go into minute detail and show every single item of expenditure, you have to show the basics of your accounts on the self-assessment return, including a broad brush break down of expenses that you are claiming against your turnover. You will also need to file your paper return by 31 October and your online return by 30 December, assuming you wish to pay the tax through your PAYE code, otherwise by 31 January.

### Case Study Alice

Alice starts her business on 1 August 2010 and decides on a 31 July year-end rather than adopt the fiscal year. To simplify matters, she earns £3,000 a month (£36,000 a year). Under the starting year rules, she must account for her business from August to the following 31 March (eight months) in her 2010–11 return due by 31 January 2012. This sounds reasonable. But under the overlap regulations, her second year-end is more than 12 months from the start of trading. So she also has to account for the 12-month period to 31 July 2011 as well – resulting in having to pay tax on 20 months financed by 12 months trading. In this example, she has had to pay tax twice on the same 12 months. Alice would have done better sticking to the fiscal year. Alice would have needed strong reasons for non-fiscal year accounting – or was badly advised.

as late as 31 January 2012, there is a substantial gap between earning the money and paying the taxes.

Many accountants recommend this non-fiscal year accounting. But there are drawbacks – especially in the first two years – that may discourage you from this. Your first year's tax bill is based on your actual profits from the day you start until the next 5 April. Taxes in the next year are calculated either on the

12 months of trading that ends on your chosen date – or your first 12 months of trading.

This is known as '**overlap**' and can result in the same profits being taxed twice. You won't normally get this 'overlap' back until you cease self-employment and this will not be adjusted for inflation or any change of tax rates.

Opting for a non-fiscal year tends to only make sense these days if your first period is likely to be loss-making where there is no profit to tax or if profits are anticipated to rise significantly in later years (see also the Ask the expert box, overleaf, on what to do when you lose money).

## Jargon buster

**Overlap** Where the accounting year you have chosen and the official tax year do not coincide - it can mean complicated and sometimes higher tax bills when you start out

**Payment on account** Amounts you pay HMRC via your self-assessment form for future earnings - even though you have not yet collected them from your customers

## CLOSING YOUR SELF-EMPLOYED BUSINESS

Just as there are complex rules when you start, there are also rules when you finish your business. Besides reversing any overlap you have paid, you pay the tax through two **payments on account** (see page 75) and a final tax payment or refund on 31 January following the end of the tax year.

For the tax year you close down, you are taxed on your profits from the accounting date on which tax for the previous year was based up to the date of closure less any overlap profits brought forward. If your accounting date is early in the tax year, this means you may have had to have paid tax on nearly two years' worth of profits in one tax year earlier on. If overlap profits have been carried forward many years, they may reduce your taxable profits very little.

Again, opting for fiscal accounting can simplify matters. You can also change your tax year to the fiscal year during the life of your business – it may be simpler than waiting until you cease trading.

**❝Opting for fiscal accounting can simplify matters. You can change your tax year to the fiscal year during the life of your business.❞**

 The section 'Coming off self-assessment' on pages 189–90 gives further advice on what you need to do when closing a self-employed business.

## What happens when you make a loss?

No one sets out in any business to make a loss. But often the first year or years may result in a deficit – there are start-up costs and advertising may not work for a time. In addition, you may simply experience a bad year – work depending on the weather, for example, can be battered by storms or snow. There are two options you can take if you make a loss once you have deducted all your allowable expenses from your takings.

The first choice is to subtract it from other taxable income or that year and/or the previous tax year – your earnings from employment, a pension, dividends or interest or capital gains where you would have to pay tax. Someone earning £25,000 from a PAYE job and having a £2,000 loss on their self-employment would see their taxable earnings for the year fall to £23,000. As they will have already paid tax on their job through PAYE, this should give a rebate of £400 (£2,000 x 20 per cent).

You can stretch this choice when you start up. If you make a loss in any of the first four years, you can offset this loss against your salary in the three preceding years, with the earliest year first. As an anti-avoidance measure, tax inspectors will want to ensure the loss-making business is genuine, not a loss-making 'hobby' and it intends to make an eventual profit. To do this, you must inform HMRC within 12 months following the 31 January after the end of your loss-making business year.

Alternatively, if your losses exceed other taxable sums (perhaps you have not worked before), you can carry the loss forward against your future expected profits. You can do this year after year if you have to – there is no time limit here but you must inform the tax authorities within five years after the 31 January in which your accounting year ended.

In general, the first option gives more immediate results but the second may be useful if you expect to go from loss making into substantial profits. Where possible, offset your losses against income that has been taxed at the top 40 per cent rate rather than at a lower rate.

See HMRC helpsheet IR227 'Losses' for more details.

## CHANGE OF WORK

Each different form of work that you do requires its own set of accounts. And if you cease one but carry on another, then you have to use the rules on page 73 for closing a business.

> **"** The cost of wages you pay your partner, older children and other family members will be deducted from your profits as expenses. **"**

---

**Case Study** **Jo and Ann**

Jo spends half her week gardening and the other half as an artist. She has two distinct businesses with no linking between them so she needs two sets of accounts.

Ann is a plumber and electrician. These two trades are close enough – she can use the same van, advertise the two skills together and buy in goods from the same suppliers. So she only has to send in one set of accounts – she will probably refer to herself as a 'handywoman' business.

---

## PAYMENTS ON ACCOUNT

You normally pay tax on self-employment earnings via the self-assessment form in two instalments – by 31 January and 31 July each year. But the basis of the two-payments-a-year system is that you pay tax on both income you have received and on income you will receive during the next tax year. This latter payment is 'on account'.

## YOUR FAMILY ON THE PAYROLL

You can legitimately put your partner, older children and other family members on the payroll. The cost of the wages you pay them will be deducted from your profits as expenses so your overall tax bill will be reduced. If the family member's total earnings (including what you pay) is below the Personal Allowance, he or she will pay no Income Tax. Alternatively, if you are a top-rate taxpayer and your partner (or another family member) is a basic-rate taxpayer, then employing them to do some work would cut the overall tax burden on the household (and free up some time for you!).

But there are rules to follow. The most vital is that the work has to be real and the remuneration in line with genuine commercial wage rates. And it has to be paid. Tax inspectors may check – so ensure there is a record of the money

---

For more information on payments on account, see pages 191-3, which explains when, how and what you pay.

leaving your bank account and going into that of the family member.

Whatever the annual earnings of the family member, you would be liable to pay employer's National Insurance and deduct employee's National Insurance whenever the weekly earnings went over the lower earnings limit (£97 a week in 2010–11). Where a piece of occasional work is worth £150, it can be worthwhile splitting the time over two weeks to stay below the level.

Before employing under-16s, always check with your local council. Rules affecting those of compulsory school age when they work vary from area to area. This applies especially to work outside the home.

“Before employing under-16s, always check with your local council as rules affecting those of compulsory school age when they work vary from area to area.”

 If you are paying your children to work for you there is more information concerning the tax implications on pages 92-8.

# Other taxes you might pay

In addition to paying Income Tax on your profits, you might also have to pay National Insurance and Value Added Tax (VAT) as a result of your self-employment.

## NATIONAL INSURANCE PAYMENTS

If you are under State Pension age you may be liable for National Insurance payments if you are self-employed. There are two types of National Insurance that might apply – Class 2 and Class 4 (see pages 56–7). There are limits on the amount of National Insurance you have to pay if you have more than one source of earnings. You should not have to pay Class 2 if you have employment where you are paying regular Class 1 payments from your salary or wages. This should be adjusted automatically.

Neither should you have to pay Class 4 if you have already paid the maximum National Insurance for the year (£43,875 in 2010–11 on earnings) from an employer. This does not include the surcharge, however, which is not given automatically.

If you believe you might be charged twice, write to HMRC via your local tax office and apply for 'deferment' – HMRC speak for not having to pay National Insurance. Someone with a PAYE salary of £45,000 a year and £10,000 from self-employment could apply for deferment as the salary already takes the taxpayer over the National Insurance

upper earnings level. But someone with £20,000 in PAYE salary and the same £10,000 from self-employment will have to pay Class 4 on the self-employment profits above the lower earnings level.

> **If you are under State Pension age and are self-employed, you may be liable for National Insurance payments – Classes 2 and 4.**

### Tax tip

You should stop paying National Insurance when you reach state retirement age – 65 for a man, and 60 to 65 (rising from 2010 to 2015 (see page 16)) for a woman, on earnings from self-employment. To do this, tick box 3.94 in the self-employment pages of the tax return to ensure you are not billed for National Insurance.

## VALUE ADDED TAX

Most taxes hit the profit you make when you sell something or where you earn money. But value added tax (VAT) is different. This is a tax on sales or turnover and, if you are registered for it, you will usually have to charge customers and clients 17.5 per cent on top of the bill they would otherwise pay.

You must register for VAT if the annual turnover of your business exceeds £68,000. This applies whether you are a sole trader, in a partnership or run a limited company. This VAT threshold usually changes each year, rising roughly in line with inflation.

There are special rules to prevent VAT dodging that ensure firms with a turnover in any one quarter higher than 25 per cent of the annual threshold also have to register. This stops seasonal traders starting a company, which perhaps sells £50,000 of goods in a quarter, shutting it down after three months and then setting up another company – and another.

 You have to register if your turnover is large enough even though all the goods you sell are zero-rated. Failing to register within 30 days of being aware your sales have passed the limit brings a fine of the greater of £50 or 5 per cent of the VAT owed – on top of the VAT itself. This percentage fine goes up to 10 per cent after 9 months and 15 per cent after 18 months.

## HOW TO PAY VAT

There are four main ways to pay VAT and reclaim the VAT on goods and services you buy in. The first is really for big companies; the latter three were purpose-designed for smaller businesses.

### Standard quarterly reporting

This is the system used by big companies and is usually where most VAT-registered traders start. Here you add up all the 'outputs' – the invoices sent to customers (whether paid or not) during the quarter and calculate the tax due on these.

**❝ You must register for VAT if the annual turnover of your business exceeds £68,000. ❞**

 For information on the different rates of VAT and what goods are zero-rated, see pages 17-18. See also www.which.co.uk/advice/your-money/ for information on tax updates.

## Ask the expert

### Should I register for VAT if I don't need to?

Traders have to register for VAT if their turnover exceeds £68,000. And they should register if there is a good chance it will hit that figure, even if it is currently a little below that – if only to avoid fines and penalties for non-registration.

VAT traders can escape the VAT system if their turnover drops below the 'deregistration level' – this is usually set at £2,000 below the registration threshold. You can therefore now deregister at a £66,000 turnover. This is probably not worth considering if the fall in trading is likely to be temporary – perhaps you decided to take an extended holiday this year or fell ill – as you will only have to go through all the trouble of re-registering at a later date when you'll have to have new stationery because your VAT number will change.

But for those whose turnover either is or falls below – and is likely to stay below – the limit, registration is optional.

So, where I have the choice, what should I do?

It depends on what you do. Being VAT registered usually means you have to add 17.5 per cent to bills. If you deal solely or mainly with end consumers – the general public – rather than other trading organisations, the extra percentage could make you uncompetitive. Consumers (or non-VAT registered traders or other end-users such as schools) have to pay the tax and cannot reclaim it.

But if you supply goods or services to another VAT registered trader (and that takes in most large and medium-sized companies and other organisations), then you should consider registration. As they can reclaim the VAT you charge, it makes no difference to them whether you are registered or not – for some, registration is a plus point as it implies you are a certain size.

At the same time, as a VAT-registered trader, you can reclaim all the VAT you pay on what you 'input' – that's the goods and services you buy in to make your business work. The disadvantage is that you have a form to fill in – but that is not nearly so difficult if you opt for one of the schemes aimed at smaller firms (see overleaf).

You then add up all the tax on all the inputs during the same period (whether or not you have paid them) and subtract this from the output tax. If the output tax is greater than the input tax you are claiming back, you pay HMRC. But when the inputs are greater (often the case if your business only supplies zero-rated goods, such as a children's clothes shop), HMRC will send you a cheque.

The advantage of this method is that it ensures you (or an accountant) look at your finances once a quarter. The drawback is that you have to pay tax on invoices for which you have not yet necessarily been paid. Reclaiming this if your client or customers turns out to be a bad debt can be difficult.

## Cash accounting

This is for small businesses and is one step away from the standard method. It is still quarterly but you only pay on tax you have successfully collected. So there is no problem in reclaiming the tax on bad debts. You can only claim on inputs you have actually paid for.

## Annual accounting

This is aimed at businesses with annual turnovers of up to £1.35 million. The idea is that it lets traders pay 'little and often'. You agree an annual amount of VAT with HMRC based on your previous trading experience and then divide that figure by nine. You pay one of these instalments each month for nine months. You then calculate your actual trading experience for the year. This will result in either paying a balancing sum to HMRC or applying for a refund. The advantage is that you can plan your cash flow ahead for most of the year. And, if trading changes dramatically, you can opt to alter the payments.

**❝ There are four main ways to pay and reclaim VAT: standard quarterly reporting, cash accounting, annual accounting and the flat-rate scheme. ❞**

# Flat-rate scheme

This is the easiest method for those who are either 'voluntary' VAT-registered because their turnover is below the compulsory threshold or who have a turnover below £100,000 (not including VAT) when they join this scheme. It only applies as long as annual sales remain below £150,000 (unusually this figure does include VAT).

With the flat-rate scheme, you avoid having to account for VAT on all the purchases and supplies (inputs) that you make for your business and instead you calculate your bill by applying a percentage to the tax paid amounts. This percentage varies according to your trade. So you cannot claim the VAT back on individual items but neither do you have to show what you spent. If you spend very little on inputs, this can work out better.

The flat-rate percentage depends on the trade sector into which a business falls. There is a wide spread of applicable percentages ranging from 2 per cent (for food retailers) to 14.5 per cent for some building contractors (see VAT notice 733).

 You will still need to keep all your bills as records to claim them as expenses from your self-employment earnings.

---

## Case Study | Rachael

Rachael is a private investigator. Her VAT-inclusive earnings amount to £11,750 in a quarter. Under the standard scheme she would pay VAT at 17.5 per cent (£1,750) less the VAT on her expenses (inputs). But as Rachael spends her working time following errant husbands on behalf of wives suing for divorce, her VAT-able inputs are few (camera, notebook and pen) and she could not claim anyway against VAT for her train and taxi travel (as these are VAT-free).

So Rachael opts to join the flat-rate scheme. The percentage for her trade is 10 per cent. She then sends HMRC a cheque for £1,175 (10 per cent of her VAT inclusive turnover). This is up to £635 less than she would otherwise have paid. Furthermore, Rachael has saved a lot of time in working out her VAT and filing in her VAT form.

She can change her mind, and revert to claiming for expenses. She can also make a special claim for the purchase of an item worth £2,000 or more. In her case, perhaps it could be a sophisticated GPS system to help track people's movements or a state-of-the-art bugging device. This is called the 'capital goods scheme'.

You add together all your outputs – the bills your customers pay – over a quarter including the VAT. You then pay HMRC a percentage of this to settle the bill quarterly. The lower the percentage, the less VAT you pay. If you join this scheme, your customers will be unaware of the decision and they will be able to claim VAT (where applicable) if they have a VAT number. You must pay electronically if your turnover tops £100,000.

You can also make a separate VAT claim for capital assets with a VAT-exclusive price of £2,000 or more – machinery or a computer, for example – except where these goods are to be sold or hired out or leased. This means you will not miss out if you buy a substantial item for your business.

## BUSINESS RATES

You will be liable to pay business rates to your local council on premises you use mostly for business. This should not affect you if you work from home – unless you have substantially changed the residential nature of your property. Changes could include using much of the property as a warehouse or having a large number of clients or customers visiting you at home. If you do change your home to this extent, you may have to apply for planning permission.

**❝If you work from home, you shouldn't have to pay business rates unless you have changed the residential nature of your property.❞**

 To find out more about each of these schemes, go to http://customs.hmrc.gov.uk and then click on the Information and Guides tab, and open the link Special Schemes and Options.

# Becoming a company

Many self-employed people consider setting themselves up as a company. This can appear attractive, but there are plus points and drawbacks from a tax point of view.

Many small businesses have 'incorporated' – the technical term for setting yourself up as a limited company – over the past decade. Some have taken this route as it would appear to confer 'big business' status on what may be effectively a one-person band. Others like the idea of calling themselves a 'company director'. But the majority were attracted down the company route by a series of apparent tax concessions that treated limited companies, no matter how small, better than self-employed sole traders, even when their businesses were otherwise identical.

HMRC has been looking at the question of how to ensure tax equality between sole trader status, partnerships and limited companies for some time. But, as in so many other items in this book, while it is important to consider the tax implications of what you do, you should never let the tax tail wag the business dog.

## ADVANTAGES OF LIMITED COMPANY STATUS

The advantages of becoming a limited company are:

- You can keep profits in the business rather than having to pay them out to a sole trader or partner. Corporation Tax on profits is generally lower than Income Tax for individuals or partners.
- You can pay those who backed the company (including the directors) via share capital with dividend payments. Dividend payments do not attract National Insurance bills so there is an advantage for company directors.

> **❝** Although it is obviously always important to consider tax implications of decisions you make, you should never let the tax tail wag the business dog. **❞**

**Jargon buster**

**Corporation Tax** An annual tax levied on the profits of companies

Dividends that you pay out are taxed at a special small company 19 per cent rate and they are considered as fully paid from the tax point of view for basic-rate taxpayers (who would otherwise pay 20 per cent Income Tax).

- It can be easier from the tax point of view to sell an incorporated business when you retire or die than a sole trading firm or a partnership.
- Ambitious company owners can raise money from outside shareholders via the Enterprise Investment Scheme, which gives tax breaks to investors in small unquoted companies.
- Your business tax affairs become separate from your personal tax affairs. As a director, you draw a salary from your company – you can limit this to avoid paying top-rate tax or the additional National Insurance surcharge.

## "Company accounts and fees may outweigh the tax benefits of a company. "

## REASONS NOT TO GO DOWN THE COMPANY ROUTE

However, there are also reasons not to become a limited company:

- You have to make National Insurance payments both as an employer and as an employee if you draw a salary above about £100 a week.
- Dividends do not count as earnings for pension contribution purposes.
- Company pension schemes can be complex and no longer have the advantages they once had for small incorporated firms.
- Accounts may be more complicated and costly to produce. They will generally have to be audited and you cannot escape a full set of accounts, even if your turnover is low – unlike sole traders who do not have to file more than a brief summary of turnover and profits if their sales are low (see pages 69–70).
- You have to pay annual fees to Companies House, which may outweigh any tax benefits in some instances.

# Tax and your family

Tax should never rule the head – or the heart. But however big or small your family might be, it pays to know how the tax rules work both to maximise your potential tax savings and to avoid running foul of tax law.

4

# To marry or not to marry?

HMRC recognises marriage as an institution. And since December 2005, civil partnerships have been recognised as well - all tax law was rewritten at that time to give equality to both forms of union. But, controversially for some, unmarried heterosexual relationships do not count for tax purposes although they are considered equivalent to marriage for some means-tested state benefits.

## GETTING ENGAGED

Your engagement has no relevance for HMRC. But once you inform the world that you intend to tie the knot – whether you have a formal engagement or not – you can tell your parents, grandparents, other relations and friends that wedding presents they give you up to the day you actually get married could escape their estate even if they die within seven years. This is not very romantic. But it could be realistic. This exemption does not count once the wedding day is over.

### Rewrite your will

Any will you may have written in the past becomes invalid on marriage. A well-drafted will can help minimise any IHT should you die. You can both write a new will in anticipation of your new legal relationship – you do not have to wait until after the ceremony.

## MARRIAGE AND CIVIL PARTNERSHIP

Same-sex couples get the same treatment when it comes to tax as married couples, as long as they have formed a civil partnership under the Civil Partnership Act. You and your partner or spouse each has your own allowance and is taxed independently, even if one of you pays tax and the other doesn't.

This means that each of you is entitled to the first slice of your income free of tax – £6,475 in 2010–11 – but you can't transfer any unused portion of the allowance to your legal partner, even if it is unused. That said, partners may be able to reduce their overall tax charge by moving assets between the two of them. Recent IHT tax rule changes (see pages 144–62) mean the estates of those who are

For more information on what you can and can't give away relating to IHT, see pages 148-60. See also the *Which? Essential Guide* to *Wills and Probate* for guidance on writing - and rewriting - your will.

legally married and in a civil partnership can benefit automatically from two sets of allowances on their death. Living together does not permit the transfer of the IHT allowance from one to the other.

## Individual investments

If one of you pays tax at a higher rate, a simple way to save tax is to transfer some investments to the person paying the lower rate or paying no tax at all. This works if one of you pays at 40 per cent and the other partner pays basic-rate tax (20 per cent on savings), or where the whole income is covered by the Personal Allowance. And where one of you is on the very top 40 per cent rate and the partner is not a taxpayer, it can potentially save the most.

## Putting an account in joint names

The disadvantage of transferring an asset from one partner to the other is that the partner who gives the asset away loses any use of it. But if you arrange for holding it jointly, you can both access the asset – useful if it is money in a bank or building society account. Holding an account in joint names need not impose any constraints on who withdraws what (unless you set up an account where it needs both to sign for a withdrawal). If you have investments in joint names, you'll each pay tax on half the resulting income, even if you originally owned them in unequal shares.

**To make any of the transfer arrangements described between spouses or civil partners work, you have to trust your other half. These will only work if you legally transfer the savings account, shares or other assets either wholly or in part to your partner. Once you have done this, you no longer have any ownership or control rights over the asset. These assets would count as part of your partner's wealth if your relationship ended. You can only get them back provided your other half agrees to the transfer – but that would end the tax benefits of gifting the assets to your partner.**

**Case Study** **Patrick and Henry**

Patrick and Henry entered into a civil partnership in 2005. Patrick has no income. Henry is a 40 per cent taxpayer. Henry has a £100,000 savings account paying 3 per cent interest – an annual £3,000, reduced by tax to £1,800. He gives the whole account to Patrick who can then either register for tax-free interest using form R85 (see page 93) or make a claim to recover tax after it is deducted by the bank. As the whole £3,000 falls within Patrick's annual Personal Allowance, it is completely tax free. This gains the couple £1,200.

It is comparatively rare for jointly owned assets to be split anything other than 50/50. One possibility might be shares in a family company where control is as important as ownership. But where that is so, then the tax will be levied in that same, unequal, proportion.

If you would prefer to be taxed on the actual proportion you own, tell HMRC. You can't have the income taxed unequally just because you think it would be to your advantage – the investment must actually be held in unequal shares. If you jointly own shares in your own company, they are always taxed in line with the proportion in which you own them.

## Married Couple's Allowance

Married couples in general now receive no extra Income Tax benefit (although there are possible tax savings from the tax-free transfer of assets between spouses and civil partners). But if you or your partner were born before 6 April 1935 and you are legally married or in a registered civil partnership, you can apply for the Married Couple's Allowance. This date does not and will not alter – unless one of you was born before it, you will never be able to apply for it (unless the tax rules change substantially some time in the future). The Married Couple's Allowance can reduce your overall tax bill.

The Married Couple's Allowance generally goes to the husband in a heterosexual relationship and the higher paid partner in a lesbian or gay relationship. Every couple receives a basic amount and, depending on who earns what, the recipient can split the allowance with the partner or give it all to the partner. You have to make this decision before the start of the tax year – other than in the tax year when you marry or contract a civil partnership, when you have until the end of the tax year in question to make this choice. You can only claim for the months of your legally sanctioned relationship during the year in which you contract the marriage or civil partnership.

---

**Case Study** **Sam and Jacqueline**

Sam and Jacqueline receive the allowance. Sam's earnings are very low so he transfers all the basic allowance to her. For the current tax year, this amounts to £2,670. Provided Jacqueline has sufficient income she can reduce her tax bill by 10 per cent of the £2,670, so she pays £267 less in 2010-11. If she did not earn enough over her Personal Allowance to absorb the entire £2,670, then she would claim 10 per cent of her total tax bill back.

---

### Married Couple's Allowance

| Maximum levels (2010-11) | |
| --- | --- |
| Under 75 | 10 per cent of £6,865 |
| Over 75 | 10 per cent of £6,965 |
| Minimum levels (2010-11) | |
| All qualifying ages | £2,670 |

## Ask the expert

### How do I claim?

Simply telephone or write to your tax office with details of your marriage/civil partnership ceremony. If you have been married for some time, this should be given to you automatically – but ensure you fill in section 16 on the self-assessment form if you have one. This is also where you can transfer some or all of your allowance to your partner.

There is a second level of payment whose payment (if any) depends on the income of the husband or higher paid civil partner. This cannot be transferred between partners.

Confusingly, the Married Couple's Allowance is different to the personal or age-related Personal Allowance. Those latter allowances allow you to earn more without falling into the tax net. The Married Couple's Allowance gives you a discount on the first slice of taxable income instead. This discount is equal to 10 per cent of the tax you would otherwise pay on the amount of the allowance.

The amount you are entitled to depends on the age of the older partner,

## Ask the expert

### Are there any benefits from remaining unhitched?

Generally speaking, most of the tax advantages go to those who have legally tied their union. If you're cohabiting, whatever your sexual orientation, there are several crucial drawbacks:

- You can't claim the Married Couple's Allowance under any circumstances.
- The surviving partner has no automatic right of inheritance when one of you dies. If you don't make a will, relatives other than your partner inherit your estate. You cannot transfer assets at death outside of IHT. That could mean a virtually open-ended loss – the better off you are, the more you stand to gain from

the ability to move assets from one to the other.
- You may have to pay CGT if you transfer assets between the pair of you (see pages 134–42).

But unmarried partners can profit as both can own a home as their main residence, which they could sell free of CGT concerns. Couples who marry or contract a civil partnership can only have one main residence between them, even if both owned a home beforehand. There is a maximum three-year window in which one property can be sold without a CGT liability. Otherwise, the couple has to decide which of their properties they want to list as their main residence.

that of the younger partner and the income of the recipient. Every relationship can claim the basic amount – £2,670 – but many recipients can claim the maximum amount – £6,965. Both these figures rise slightly when the recipients have passed their 75th birthday (see the allowance table on page 88).

The maximum Married Couple's Allowance starts to erode at different income levels. If the income falls between the higher and the lower points, then there is a £1 reduction in the enhanced level allowance for every extra £2 that is earned – just as with age-related Personal Allowance. This can give rise to a trap, but as the Married Couple's Allowance is only worth 10 per cent, it is not as dramatic as the age allowance trap can be. When one of you dies, the allowance stops, but if one or both of you go into hospital or a residential home, the tax benefit continues.

## Inheritance Tax (IHT)

All gifts and other transfers between spouses and civil partners are free of IHT. However, if you leave some or all of your estate to the other person without tax planning, you could lose out on some potential savings because you won't be using both your IHT-free allowances

## Case Study Michael and Christine and George and Sue

Michael and Christine, a married couple, own a £500,000 house and £650,000 in investments. Michael dies leaving everything to Christine (her will would have left everything to him had she died first). When she dies, her estate will be able to claim twice whatever the IHT allowance is at the time. If she dies in 2010, it will be £650,000 (twice the £325,000 for this year). Assuming the value of the home and investments stay unchanged, the IHT bill will be £500,000 at 40 per cent giving a £200,000 bill. Michael's allowance is used fully without complex trusts.

George and Sue have a home and investments of the same value as Michael and Christine. George leaves £300,000 (the IHT allowance for 2009, the year he died) to his children. There is no tax to pay, but this exhausts the allowance. When Sue dies in 2010, her estate claims her £325,000 allowance. As a result, the couple has only had £625,000 in allowances - £25,000 less than Michael and Christine. Their estate has to pay £10,000 more in tax than the other couple's.

to their best advantage (see pages 148–60). You can help overcome this in some circumstances using an easily available form of trust combined with the correct wording for your wills. You should seek professional advice on this.

## Capital Gains Tax (CGT)

Every individual has an annual tax-free allowance (£10,100 in 2010–11), which can be against any CGT bills that you might have to pay when you sell certain assets, including businesses at a profit.

Couples whether married or co-habiting effectively have two allowances. But the big difference is that co-habitees cannot transfer assets between each other without facing a potential CGT bill if the disposal from one to the other is profitable.

Married and civil partnership couples can, however, move assets from one to the other at any time up to the moment the asset is sold. So by dividing the asset in two (or in whatever other ratio works best to maximise the allowance) they can benefit from two sets of capital gain allowances – £20,200 – against the eventual sale.

But you cannot use this transfer between partners to create a loss. Unmarried couples can create a loss when they move an asset between them – this can be useful if one unmarried partner could use a CGT loss but not the other.

## Getting divorced

While the general law says that divorcing couples only end their relationship with the decree absolute, HMRC only allows CGT-free transfers in a tax year when the splitting partners have lived together for at least part of the year. Otherwise, the transfers would be liable to CGT, causing problems for ex-partners who are trying to sort out their assets as part of their break-up settlement.

## Maintenance payments

Any maintenance payments your estate continues to make to a former spouse or civil partner or for the upkeep and education of a child of your former relationship until they are 18 or are still in full-time education are outside the IHT net if you die. Money you receive as maintenance or from the child support agency is tax free – it will have been taxed as part of the earnings of the former partner who is paying the money.

You can only claim tax relief in maintenance payments you make if you or your ex-partner were born before 6 April 1935. The most you can claim is the lower of either the amount you pay or £2,670 in 2010–11. Relief is given as a 10 per cent reduction in your tax bill, giving a maximum reduction of £267 in 2010–11.

**Case Study  Doreen and Daniel**

Doreen and Daniel last lived together on 15 April before they split. They have until the following 5 April to sort out their assets without paying CGT. Had they broken up a few days earlier on 4 April, they would have had only one day in which to divide their assets tax free.

# Children

You become a potential taxpayer the moment you are born. And you also qualify for a personal Income Tax allowance from that moment. Few children have enough earnings from work to use all the allowance. So with careful use, the child's tax allowance can help boost the family's overall fortune.

## FORM R85 – THE ROUTE TO TAX-FREE SAVINGS

Children have the same tax-free allowance as an adult (£6,475 in 2010–11), but they rarely use this up with earnings. So they generally have the allowance available to set against other income – largely interest on their savings accounts. This ensures they receive interest tax free.

The best way to make sure children do not pay tax is to complete form R85 (see box, below) when you open an account in their name (or when they are older, when they open an account for themselves). You need to fill in a form R85 for each account as well as for each bank or building society. Don't worry if you haven't done this though: if your child is paying tax, reclaim it for them by completing form R40 'Claim for Repayment'.

 While the R85 on an account continues from year to year (unless you tell HMRC that the child's earnings are such that it no longer applies), it stops in the tax year the child reaches 16, even if she or he is still in full-time education and has no additional income. If the child still qualifies for tax-free income, then she or he will have to fill in a new R85 for every savings account in her or his name.

### Tax tip

You can still collect the 10 per cent tax rate on savings interest income on the first £2,440 above the Personal Allowance. The savings income is counted after income from employment or self-employment.

 To download forms R85 'Getting your interest without tax taken off', and R40 'Claim for repayment', go to www.hmrc.gov.uk. For more information on child trust funds, see website www.childtrustfund.gov.uk.

# GIVING MONEY TO YOUR OWN CHILDREN

Grandparents, godparents, aunts, uncles and everyone else – other than parents – can give children as much money as they like without worrying about how much income is earned on those gifts. If the gifts are substantial though, they might need to think about IHT (see Chapter 8).

But there are low limits on the amount of money you can give to your own child where the interest will be tax free. Each parent can give money that creates up to £100 in interest before tax is deducted each year. At current interest rates, that is around £3,500 if you invest in best buy accounts. This does not matter if the children are adopted, natural, legitimate, illegitimate or live with you or not.

This '£100 rule' applies to gifts from each parent, so a child can have a tax-free income of £200 from parental gifts if both parents give equally, provided the interest from these accounts does not take the child over her or his Personal Allowance. However, once the money you give them makes more than £100 a year in interest, it will be taxed as though it were your own income and at your highest personal tax

band level. This applies to the whole interest – not just the amount above the £100 limit.

## CHILD TRUST FUNDS

All children born on or after 1 September 2002 receive at least £250 from the Government – £500 for children born into lower income families – in a child trust fund. This money has to be invested into approved funds consisting of cash or shares or bonds and cannot be normally encashed until the child reaches 18.

Your child's trust fund is first paid when you start claiming Child Benefit (a benefit available for all children irrespective of parental income). The child then receives a further £250 (or £500 for families on lower incomes) when she or he reaches seven.

For those who can afford it, the big tax-saving opportunity comes because anyone – including parents – can top up the Government payments with a further £1,200 a year. For parents, this is over and above any amount they have given that counts for the £100 annual tax-free interest limit (see above).

Parents should keep records of what they and others give their children to show which cash comes from parents and what comes from others.

93

Cash-based child trust fund accounts and those that invest in gilts and bonds can reclaim the 20 per cent tax that would otherwise be deducted. Share-based accounts lose the 10 per cent dividend tax, which cannot be reclaimed under any circumstances in any sort of fund. They do, however, offer freedom from any future CGT on an eventual sale.

## PAYMENTS TO PENSIONS

Contributing to a pension scheme on behalf of a child is another tax-efficient way of saving for them. But as your child cannot get at the money until he or she reaches the minimum age for drawing a pension, which, under present legislation, is 55, you may consider this to be unhelpful in giving your child a start in adult life. You may also not live to see them enjoy this money. You also have to bet on pension planning remaining unchanged for the best part of half a century – the previous 50 years hardly offer confidence in that respect.

But if you can cope with all that, you can pay up to £3,600 a year into a stakeholder pension on behalf of your child or anyone else's, including grandchildren. Payments qualify for the addition of tax relief into your child's pension account at the rate applicable to your child, as if he or she had made the contribution, so you would only have to pay in £2,880 to get the £3,600. At the very least, the recipient might then have to put less into their own pension plan when they reach the age of working seriously.

## CHILDCARE COSTS

If you have a child who needs paid-for childcare, check to see if your employer has a scheme (or lobby with other parents for the setting up of a plan). Your employer may offer childcare vouchers or otherwise help with the cost of childcare, for example by providing a workplace nursery.

If your employer does provide a workplace nursery (it does not have to be at the workplace itself and it can be a facility shared with other employers), you won't pay tax or National Insurance on any of the benefit; otherwise, you won't pay tax or National Insurance on the first £55 a week. It may be worth looking at a form of 'salary sacrifice' where you give up part of your earnings in return for tax-free or tax-beneficial benefits. The £55 limit applies regardless of how many children you have, but it does apply to both parents, so you could get up to £110 a week if there are two parents. The tax-free workplace nursery facility applies, no matter how many children you have.

The childcare must be provided by an approved person (such as a registered childminder), and the benefit must be available to all staff. If your employer provides childcare vouchers, they will deduct the amount you wish to claim from your salary in exchange for the voucher, which you give to your childcare provider. If you claim the full amount and are a basic-rate taxpayer, you could save more than £900 a year; higher-rate taxpayers save even more. The childcare provided does not have to be on a full-time basis – it can include 'mornings only' or 'after school' or 'school holidays only'.

# Tax Credits

In spite of their name, the only link between Tax Credits and tax is that they are both administered by HMRC. Effectively, they are a means-tested benefit designed to provide extra money for people bringing up children, disabled workers or workers on lower incomes. There are two types: Working Tax Credit (WTC) and Child Tax Credit (CTC).

You might be eligible for one or both, but whether you qualify and how much you get depends on your circumstances and income when you make the claim and in the year prior to the claim. So, if you put in a claim, it is the income you received in the most recently ended tax year (from 6 April to the following 5 April) that will be used to assess your claim. The credits are cash payments – not allowances against your tax bill. Overpayments have been the main problem to beset the Tax Credits system. If you think you have been overpaid, ask the Tax Credits Office how much and the reason. If you can't repay the money or the overpayment is because of a mistake by the Tax Credits Office, you may not have to pay it back – fill in form TC846 (see below), requesting to reconsider recovery of Tax Credits.

## Watch your income year-to-year, not week-to-week

HMRC calculates Working Tax Credit and Child Tax Credit on a year-to-year-earnings basis. This replaces former means-tested benefits, which were worked out on a week-to-week basis.

This can create difficulties for those with sharply fluctuating earnings – either of not claiming when income falls or failing to report rising income. In the latter case, HMRC has, often controversially, pursued claimants for substantial overpayments.

You must report all annual household income increases of £25,000 or more at once, so you don't have to tell HMRC about every single change.

 Download form TC846 'Tax credits overpayment' from www.hmrc.gov.uk or contact Citizens Advice (www.citizensadvice.org.uk) for help.

## CHILD TAX CREDIT (CTC)

You do not have to be working to claim the CTC and any benefit is in addition to Child Benefit payments. To be eligible, you must have at least one dependant child and a household income (taking in both parents in a two-parent family) of less than £58,000 a year (£66,000 if the child is below the age of one). If you earn more than this but have substantial childcare costs, you may still be eligible, so it could still be worth making a claim. The income figure includes everything – not just earnings from work.

Provided your household income is under the maximum level, you should receive at least the 'basic family element' of £545 per year – this doubles to £1,090 for families with a baby under

### Tax tip

The HMRC website has a calculator so you can see if you are eligible and, if so, how much you might get. Go to www.taxcredits.inlandrevenue.gov.uk/Qualify/DIQHousehold.aspx.

one. Up to £2,300 can be paid for each additional child, depending on income, and there are also payments if you are responsible for a child with a disability, which can reach £2,715. For full details of what you might receive, see HMRC leaflet WTC2 'Child tax credit and working tax credit'. The basic £545 is known as the 'family element' – the amount for the first year of a child's life is called 'family element, baby addition'.

You can only receive one family element no matter how many children there are – if one is a baby, the family element will be paid at the higher rate for that year.

## WORKING TAX CREDIT (WTC)

WTC is for people on moderate to low incomes, regardless of whether they have children, and can be paid in addition to CTC. To claim, you must work at least 30 hours a week, be 25 or older and have an income below £11,800 a year if you are single, or £16,400 jointly if you are in a couple and childless. If you are disabled and work or have children, you may qualify if you earn more than this. For more information, see HMRC leaflet WTC2 'Child tax credit and working tax credit'.

### Ask the expert

#### How do I claim?

Although CTC in one form or another applies to the great majority of families, you have to apply for it as HMRC does not add up both incomes in a two-parent household for any other reason. It is means-tested, not a universal benefit, such as Child Benefit.

You can ask your local tax office for a form and claim pack, you can find details online at hmrc.gov.uk/taxcredits, or you can call the CTC helpline on 0845 300 3900 (or 0845 603 2000 in Northern Ireland).

You must do this as soon as possible. You can continue to claim for someone aged 16-19 years of age if they are still in full-time school, sixth form college or similar education (but not at university or a similar institution).

If you fail to claim or let your claim lapse, you can only claim three months back retrospectively – unlike the six years HMRC can have to chase you for overpayments.

Everyone who qualifies gets the basic element, worth up to £1,920, depending on your income. You might also receive extra elements depending on your circumstances – for example, if you are a lone parent, a disabled worker or spend money on approved childcare.

## Extra elements

If you are a lone parent, payments are always made to those who qualify who have responsibility for his or her child or children (see the case study, below) – neither the payments nor the means testing involve the absent parent. Lone parents are more likely to qualify as their earnings may be lower than that of two parents living together.

You must make a new claim both for CTC and WTC (generally paid via your employer if you are in low paid work) when you end your relationship – or embark on a new one.

If you are disabled: you get extra WTC provided:

- You work at least 16 hours a week,
- Your income is low enough,
- You get certain disability benefits and

### Case Study Jacqueline

Jacqueline is the single parent mother of two children Sadie, 11 and Brett, 7. She earns around £300 a week, and her childcare costs (using local authority approved child care) are £90 a week. She applies for WTC because she is lower paid. The calculation gives her the following per week:

| | |
|---|---|
| Child Tax Credit | £97 |
| Childcare element of WTC | £72 |
| WTC adjusted for the childcare element | £18 |
| Total per week addition | £187 |

Jacqueline would not get this money had she not applied for WTC. The amount paid will change depending on her salary or childcare costs; they will also be adjusted if her family circumstances change. The sum change each year - these figures are based on 2010-11 figures. They have been rounded for simplicity.

- Your disability puts you at a disadvantage in getting a job.

HMRC may ask you to give them the name of a healthcare professional who can confirm how your disability affects your chances of finding work. This might be a doctor, occupational therapist or a community nurse.

The qualifying benefits include Incapacity Benefit, Disability Living Allowance, Employment and Support

Allowance, Attendance Allowance, Industrial Injuries Disablement Benefit, Statutory Sick Pay, a war pension with constant attendance allowance, occupational sick pay or Income Support or National Insurance credits awarded because you have been unable to work. There are two levels of disability additions for WTC, which in 2010–11 are:

- The standard disability element: £2,570.
- The severe disability element: an additional £1,095 to the standard disability element.

## CHECK YOUR AWARD

When you get notification of your award, check it, and appeal against it if you think it is wrong. Ask HMRC for an explanation if you think your Tax Credit award is wrong, and if you still don't agree, you can appeal against the decision, although you must contact the Tax Credits Office within one month of receiving your award notice. You must be able to show you were unaware that the money was paid in error. This is not always easy.

### Tax tip

You do not declare any Tax Credits you have received on your tax form.

## Renewing your claim

You will get a renewal pack each year, and if your details haven't changed significantly, you should just affirm they are correct and return the completed renewal by the deadlines. But if your circumstances have changed, tell HMRC immediately to prevent overpayment or underpayment problems.

## OTHER HELP IF YOU GET TAX CREDITS

If you are claiming Tax Credits because you are on a low income, or you have children, you may be entitled to other support from the Government – this is often called 'passporting'.

- You can get help with certain health costs, such as NHS prescriptions, dental treatment and optical vouchers.
- Pregnant women can claim food supplements under the Healthy Start Scheme.
- The Sure Start maternity grant gives £500 for each baby to those who qualify.
- You may get help with school meals, uniforms and cost of school travel.
- You may also get help with court fees, legal costs, prison visits, metered water charges in England and Wales, essential house repairs or improvements and home energy efficiency schemes.

 For more about the Healthy Start Scheme go to www.healthystart.nhs.uk and the Sure Start website is www.surestart.gov.uk.

# Pensions and retirement

Most people need to save up during their working lives for income in their retirement years. Many decisions will involve tax considerations, especially joining pension plans, as these have a number of valuable tax concessions. There are, however, other investments with tax advantages to think about.

# Tax and pensions

When you are saving for retirement, it generally makes sense to start to do so in the way that attracts the greatest amount of tax generosity. The tax rules for pensions have been substantially simplified to concentrate on the pension itself rather than the type of pension you acquire.

The pensions industry paints its products as a one-way ticket to a whole host of tax benefits. What it says is true, but what it tends to relegate to the small print is the return ticket. While pension payments and pension investments benefit from a whole range of tax reliefs and concessions, HMRC will take its cut eventually when your pension plan turns into retirement savings, even if this is 50 or more years into the future.

While pensions should be the first consideration for people planning for an eventual retirement, they are not the only choice. Some, especially the lower paid, might be better advised to do nothing. Others may find it advantageous to look at other options, which offer more flexibility.

**❝ Pensions should be the first consideration when planning for retirement. ❞**

 This chapter describes the relationship currently existing between taxation and your retirement income. Pension provision is a very long-term arrangement – a 20-year-old could still be drawing a pension in 80 years time. And with increasing life expectancy, many people now aged 40 will expect pension payments in 50 or more years time. But pension and tax rules have changed many times over the past half century. There is no guarantee that they will remain the same for the next half century. This chapter sets out the tax position as it is now – not when you retire.

 Pension payments are covered on pages 105–11. Information on drawing your pension appears on pages 112–15 and alternative savings methods are discussed on page 116.

Tax savings are important, but see them in a wider context, especially if you are planning on making additional investments into a pension plan beyond the basic elements of an employer scheme.

## THE PENSIONS CHOICE

Most people's pensions are a mix of state retirement provision plus an income from plans taken out during their working lives – either employed or self-employed.

You have a limited ability to influence your basic State Pension and other state retirement payments. They are dependent on compulsory National Insurance deductions over which you normally have no control – although you can make voluntary National Insurance payments.

## National Insurance and your pension

National Insurance is an additional tax in all but name. It is paid out of your taxed income and can often be paid by those who have no Income Tax liability whatsoever in that year – typically by people doing casual or irregular work, such as students.

There are, however, some areas where your contribution record determines what state benefits you will receive. These include the basic State Pension.

"National Insurance is paid out of your taxed income."

## Tax-free state benefits for older people

Some benefits are paid without deduction of tax or any liability to tax.

- Winter Fuel Payment to help towards extra costs of keeping warm in winter. This is paid to men and women from the age of 60 at a current £250 a year. There is no means test. It is limited to £250 per household with a £150 addition where one person living in the house is 80 or over. If you are aged 60 and over and receiving a State Pension or benefit, then you should get this money (paid in late November or early December) automatically. If you are not, then you need to claim from mid August onwards (see box on page 102).
- The £10 Christmas bonus is tax free – it is usually paid along with the State Pension. This amount has been unchanged since the 1970s.
- War Widow's/Widower's Pension.
- TV licence – this is free where one person in a household has reached 75 or older.
- Attendance Allowance for help with personal care.
- Pension Credit – a means-tested benefit that tops up your income to a minimum of £130 per week for single pensioners and £198.45 for couples in 2010–11. You start to lose this benefit if your savings top £10,000.
- Travel pass for those over the female state pension age.

To qualify for the basic State Pension, you need to have paid full annual National Insurance contributions (or had them credited for reasons such as unemployment, maternity leave, or caring for someone but not for time as a student) for at least 11 years during your working life if you are retiring at 65 (ten years for women born before 6 April 1950 who can still retire at 60). You now need only 30 full years of contributions to get a full State Pension.

If you paid somewhere between the minimum and the maximum, there is a sliding scale (see the *Which? Essential Guide: Pension Handbook* for more details). Only Class 1, 2 and 3 National Insurance payments count for the sliding scale (see pages 55–7).

---

## Qualifying years

From 6 April 2010, anyone reaching State Pension age will only need 30 qualifying years for the maximum basic State Pension instead of 44 for a man and 39 for a woman. So, buying in extra years' worth of National Insurance may be money wasted – although you might still be asked if you would like to do this by HMRC.

---

Contributions from the now relatively small number paying the married women's reduced rate do not count. Equally out of contention are Class 4 payments made by the self-employed and the 1 per cent National Insurance surcharge on higher earners. There have been political moves to change payment of the basic State Pension from a contribution-records basis to a universal citizenship benefit, but for the moment, they remain just that – political moves.

## PRIVATE PROVISION

Private pensions can be financed from your own resources or from an employer or from a mix of the two. In general, they are the most tax-efficient way to save for retirement.

You either don't pay tax on the contributions you make or you can reclaim some or all of the tax on your payments later on. The pension itself can grow in a fund where most assets will not be subject to either Income Tax or CGT (although pension funds can no longer claim back tax paid on dividend payments from shares). And when you come to retire, you can take up to a quarter of your accumulated fund as a tax-free lump sum.

---

 You can get a claim form for Winter Fuel Payment by calling the Winter Fuel Payment helpline on 08459 151 515, or textphone 0845 601 5613. Lines are open Monday to Friday from 8.30am to 4.30pm. Or you can download a claim form from the Pension Service website (www.thepensionservice.gov.uk/pdf/winterfuel/bwv3jul06.pdf).

But it is worthwhile noting there can be disadvantages to pension plan savings despite the tax efficiencies.

- **Once you have made a payment** (or your employer has made a payment on your behalf), you cannot generally have a refund, even if you would rather use the money for something else, such as buying a home, starting a business or just having a good time (although you can often transfer your pension pot between pension funds). The exception to this rule is that you can have a refund of contributions you have paid into a workplace pension if you leave the scheme within two years. This refund is limited to the amount you paid in – you cannot recover contributions paid by your employer, which will then be lost. If you gain a refund, it will be adjusted for any tax relief that you may have obtained on the contributions.
- **Those with low earnings** (or potentially low earnings later in life) might be better off not paying into a plan as future payments could affect means-tested benefits, such as the Pension Credit scheme, which is administered by HMRC.

- **Tax freedom does not mean investment success.** Some pension funds have returned less than plan members contributed – there are investment risks.
- **Most plans** (other than those from an employer which promise an eventual pension based on your final salary and the number of years you spent in that scheme) **insist you buy an annuity** (an income for life) with what is left from your fund after any tax-free lump sum is deducted.

No one is currently compelled to take out a personal pension plan or to join their employer's scheme.

**"When you come to retire, you can take up to a quarter of your accumulated private pension fund as a tax-free lump sum."**

For more information on National Insurance, see pages 52-8. An explanation of the different classes of payment and what they entitle you to is given on pages 55-7. See also the *Which? Essential Guide: Finance Your Retirement*.

## Pension schemes at a glance

| Type of pension | How it works |
| --- | --- |
| Basic State Pension | Currently pays up to £97.65 a week for a single person, based on your National Insurance contribution record, not previous earnings. A partner can draw up to £58.50 in addition. |
| State Second Pension | Paid to employees on top of the basic State Pension. Earnings-related but formula more generous to lower earners than SERPS. Carers and some disabled people also qualify. |
| State Earnings Related Pension Scheme (SERPS) | Earlier earnings-related pension, replaced in 2002 by the Second State Pension. |
| Pension Credit | Main means-tested benefit for the over-60s. Provides a guaranteed minimum income of £132.60 a week for single people and £202.40 for couples from April 2010. |
| Employers' schemes (final salary) | Your employer, and usually you, pay into the scheme. Your eventual pension depends on your final salary and length of scheme membership. |
| Employers' schemes (money purchase) | You and your employer pay contributions, which are invested. Your eventual pension depends on investment performance and annuity rates. |
| Personal pension/retirement annuity contract (RAC) | A personal pension can be arranged through an employer as a group personal pension, or bought individually. Your final pension depends on investment performance and annuity rates. An RAC is an old-style personal pension arranged before mid-1988. |
| Stakeholder pension | A money purchase personal pension with capped annual charges and no charges for stopping and starting premiums or transferring. Your eventual pension depends on investment performance and annuity rates. Employers with five or more employees have to offer a stakeholder scheme although the employer is not obliged to contribute towards this. |

# Pension payments

HMRC has swept away the plethora of complicated rules that looked at your age and the exact type of pension, which determined the maximum amounts you could put into your pension. There are still limits, but these are simpler and apply only to a small, wealthy minority.

## PAYING INTO PRIVATE PENSIONS

Anyone can save into a personal pension from the day they are born to the age of 75. There is no ceiling to the actual payments you can make, but there are limits on the annual amounts paid in if you wish to collect tax relief. There are few instances where it is worth contributing to a pension if you cannot get tax relief on the way in – and these only apply to those on very high earnings. In this case, you might be better off saving for your retirement in a different way due to the drawbacks of pension plans indicated above.

## Annual contribution limits

To get tax relief, you can pay in the higher of 100 per cent of UK earnings or £3,600.

- **100 per cent of your UK earnings.** UK earnings basically means your pay and benefits from your employer if you're employed, or your taxable profits if you're self-employed. This figure includes bonuses, overtime, commissions and any other payments additional to your normal basic salary or wages. These do not have to be regular payments and they can include any freelance or spare time earning, including activities such as online trading or car boot sales. But they do not include dividends (even from your own company which you own 100 per cent and from where you have elected to take dividends instead of a salary) or interest from savings, or capital gains. You get this at your highest tax rate first (see Judith's case study, overleaf).

- **£3,600 a year.** This amount can be put into a plan either for yourself or for someone else who might not have a plan in their own right or be able to contribute to one because they have no earnings. This might include a young person or a non-working partner. Even if the recipients are not taxpayers, the contribution will attract tax relief at 20 per cent. The £3,600 is the gross amount but you do not have to find that much in cash – only that amount with the basic rate removed – £2,880. HMRC will automatically add the tax back so the pension company receives the full £3,600, which it will invest for you.

## Case Study  Judith

Judith earns £100,000 (well above the basic-rate level) and contributes £20,000 to her private pension. She therefore receives the basic rate part of her relief automatically and a refund of the gap between the basic and the higher rate. On a £20,000 payment, Judith needs to pay £16,000 in cash, which is equal to the £20,000 less 20 per cent basic-rate relief. HMRC will give her pension provider the gap between the net and the gross figure. The pension provider, however, does not know what level of tax Judith pays, but as she is in the 40 per cent tax rate, she is able to get a further £4,000 back – the 20 per cent of £20,000 that represents the difference between basic and higher 40 per cent tax rates – as tax relief is at the highest personal rate. This extra tax relief usually comes back to the taxpayer through the self-assessment form. However, Judith cannot claim back any National Insurance – and that includes the 1 per cent National Insurance surcharge on higher incomes.

## Case Study  Maria and Joanna

Maria earns £25,000 a year. Normally, she puts £1,000 a year into her personal pension plan. This is all she can afford. This year, she has been left £5,000 in her grandmother's will. She wants to boost her pension so she adds this £5,000 to her normal contribution. Although the extra money itself does not come from earnings, the £5,000 can be used to replace her normal spending money and so free up part of her salary for tax relief purposes.

Under the same will, her mother Joanna inherits £50,000. She earns £20,000 a year and currently has no pension plan contributions. The most she can put into her plan and qualify for tax relief is £20,000.

Alternatively, Joanna could spread the £30,000 balance of her inheritance over the two subsequent tax years, should she wish (and there is more to this decision than tax considerations – a good financial adviser will help). But if she does decide to put more money into her pension plan, Joanna can end up with all her inheritance in a scheme within three years should she wish.

 The National Insurance surcharge on higher incomes (see Judith's case study, above) is explained on page 16.

Top-rate taxpayers can reclaim the gap between the basic 20 per cent and the higher 40 per cent rate via their self-assessment form or HMRC form PP120, which you can get from your local tax office.

## The lifetime limit – but only for the very well off

There is a lifetime limit on the amount of pension saving that you can have that qualifies for tax relief. This figure (see table, top right) includes the value of all your pensions, whether bought by yourself or contributed by an employer, and the potential worth of any payments to your family if you die.

This lifetime allowance is calculated when you take the benefit. This is how it works:

- You start off with the limit and then you subtract all or any of the following as they are cashed in:
  - the value of any personal pensions, including the tax-free lump sum.
  - the value of any additional pensions from your employer.
  - the initial annual value of employer pensions (those based on your final salary and how long you have worked there) multiplied by 20 (for example, a £40,000-a-year plan would soak up £800,000 of the allowance).
  - lump sums payable on your death.
- What is left over is then taxed at 55 per cent on any cash lump sums you take and 25 per cent on any income you elect to take (see case study, right).

## Limits for pension funds

| Year | Lifetime limits | Annual increase |
|------|-----------------|-----------------|
| 2009-10 | £1.75 million | £245,000 |
| 2010-11 | £1.8 million | £255,000 |
| 2011-12 | to be announced | to be announced |

If you are likely to hit these limits in the future, take advice. There may be a balance between tax relief now and a future tax charge that you may wish to consider. You will also have to factor in how your fund may grow before you take the benefits.

## Case Study  George

George is a company director, earning £140,000 a year. His pension fund is already worth £1.2m. He has to calculate both his annual salary and any growth in the fund to see how much longer he can contribute to this fund. If his fund grows at 10 per cent (£120,000), then because of the annual increase limit of £255,000, he is limited to placing £135,000 of his salary, not the full amount, into his pension pot. Once he has hit the overall maximum (either for his lifetime or for a year), he will have to make other arrangements for saving up towards his retirement should he wish. His accountant may recommend an 'unapproved scheme' or other form of saving.

## The annual limit – also only for the well-off

There's also an annual limit on the amount your pension rights can increase tax free in any one year without you paying extra tax (see also the table at the top of this page). This includes both investment growth and any new contributions you might make. In most cases, the great bulk of any annual increase will come from new money paid in to your pension account.

Final salary scheme increases are measured as the actual rise in what you are promised when you retire, which is then multiplied by ten.

You have to pay a special 40 per cent tax on any amount over this annual limit. For 2010–11, the ceiling on any increase is £255,000 and you pay 40 per cent tax on any excess. This limit doesn't apply in the year before you retire.

The Government says it will monitor economic changes, including the rate of inflation, and reflect these in future increases in both the lifetime limits and the permitted annual increases.

### GETTING TAX RELIEF

How you get tax relief on contributions depends on the type of pension scheme you have – an employer-based plan or a plan that you have arranged for yourself.

## From employers' schemes

Your contributions are deducted from your pay before tax is worked out. As the money comes from the 'top line' – the gross amount you receive – it means you automatically get the right amount of tax relief. This applies whether your tax rate is at the basic- or higher-rate level. Deductions include additional voluntary contribution payments – amounts you pay extra into an employer's sponsored fund – but any payments from your employer on your behalf do not count. It does not matter if the employer plan is based on your final salary or on the fund that accumulates from the investment of your actual contributions.

The amount shown as your taxable earnings on your annual P60 form from your employer is your earnings after pension contributions.

## From personal pensions

These include **Stakeholder Pensions** you arrange for yourself and **Self-Invested Personal Pensions** (SIPPs). The amount you pay is treated as if basic-rate tax has already been deducted. The pension provider reclaims the tax and adds it back to your pension. Everyone gets this basic-rate tax relief up to the £3,600 limit, whether or not they are a taxpayer. So non- and starting-rate taxpayers get a tax bonus on their pension savings. Higher-rate taxpayers can claim extra tax relief either through their tax returns or form PP120.

The only exceptions to this rule are personal plans started before April 1988. These are known as retirement annuity contracts and you pay contributions gross and have to reclaim the relief (at your top personal rate) through the tax return. Non-taxpayers cannot reclaim the tax.

## CUTTING YOUR SALARY TO IMPROVE YOUR PENSION PAYMENTS

Here's a paradox that an increasing number of people are using – you can reduce your gross pay while increasing or at least retaining your pension payments to fund your future retirement pay – but at the same time, you actually take home more pay. It's known as **salary sacrifice** and can only work if you and your employer agree on it. And the more you earn, the more it can be worthwhile exploring this option.

What you do is to agree to earn less but ensure that the salary you have given up goes into your employer pension plan.

It works because while you have to pay National Insurance on your entire salary (including the 1 per cent surcharge where applicable), money that your employer puts into your scheme does not attract employer's National Insurance. Effectively, you are giving up money that you would normally earn to your employer, so reducing your National Insurance bill (partly offset by a loss of pension contribution relief).

Salary sacrifice can affect your eligibility for home loans (usually based on a multiple of your pre-tax earnings) and, in some cases, your future state pension. It may not be suitable for those in the final years of a final salary scheme. Always take professional advice.

Pensions and retirement

## Jargon buster

**Salary sacrifice/Sacrifice scheme** You agree with your employer to give up part of your salary in return for benefits which, because they have Income Tax or National Insurance advantages, are more valuable than the salary foregone

**Self-Invested Personal Pension (SIPP)** A plan where you control the investment

content – you can include a wide variety of assets but not residential property

**Stakeholder Pension** A government-backed scheme to provide low-cost personal pension plans. All employers with five or more staff have to offer one to their workforce but no employer is obliged to contribute to the plan

**109**

The salary you have sacrificed is then invested by the employer on your behalf, but coming from the employer itself. The figures can be complicated but it can mean both sides of the agreement are better off. Various major employers have offered sacrifice schemes – they can be used by those with a wide range of earnings from the very well off to those on average earnings or less.

## MATCHING CONTRIBUTIONS

Some employers offer to match extra contributions that you make towards your occupational pension fund. This might be on a pound-for-pound basis or a 50p-for-each-pound basis or some other ratio.

Putting more of your own money into the workplace plan when the employer recognises that with extra money is well worth thinking about – the more so if you are a higher-rate taxpayer. The maths are attractive thanks to the tax relief your own contributions attract multiplied by the employer's generosity.

A 40 per cent taxpayer in a pound-for-pound scheme pays in her or his extra pound and then receives tax relief at 40 per cent so the real cost is 60p. When the employer puts in a further £1, the pension fund member has gained £2 more for the outlay of 60p. If you fall into this category and you are old enough to draw your pension and you decide to cash in the scheme, you can get 50p of that £2 back in cash as a tax-free lump sum. That leaves £1.50 worth of pension from spending of just 10p. Of course, investment conditions will alter this arithmetic – for simplicity, the examples in this section assume the money remains unchanged.

The maths still remain attractive for the 20 per cent basic-rate taxpayer. If you are in this category, you end up paying 80p (your £1 less 20p-in-the-pound tax relief) for £2-worth of pension fund contribution. If you cashed in your plan on retirement, you would get 50p (again leaving aside investment considerations), leaving you with £1.50 in a pension plan at the cost of 30p.

For schemes that give 50p for each £1 you put in, the 40 per cent taxpayer ends up with £1.50 for a net outlay of 60p. On reaching retirement, the 25 per cent tax-free lump sum is equal to 37.5p, so this pension fund member would get £1.125 for the equivalent of 22.5p.

## FLEXIBLE BENEFITS

A growing number of employers offer flexible benefits packages where you can choose from a menu that might include extra pension, extra holiday, private medical care, a company car, or company gym membership. Employees can then mix and match to the maximum benefit level agreed with the employer. Most of these benefits are taxable because they have to be listed on your P11D annual return (see page 26), but if a pension is on 'flexi-offer', you will not be taxed.

# Special pension plans

Pensions have been substantially simplified. But there are still a number of specialist pension plans around – mostly aimed at those who either control their own business or are employed in senior positions.

There are some very specialist – and arcane – pension plans, including executive pensions and pension mortgages, but very few pension buyers have these. The main 'minority' plans are Self-Invested Personal Pensions (SIPPs) and Small Self-Administered Schemes (SSASs).

## THE SELF-INVESTED PERSONAL PENSION (SIPP)

The SIPP is effectively a personal pension with additional flexibility but with the same tax benefits as personal pensions on the way in and during the investment period. You can make your own investment decisions using a far wider variety of assets than a normal pension including commercial property (but not residential property such as buy to lets), commodities and some complex financial instruments.

They are useful in certain strategies, such as income drawdown, where you can take part of your pension fund at an earlier age leaving the final annuity decision until you reach 75. That way,

the remaining pension fund can be passed IHT-free to your family if you die before 75 (albeit the fund is taxed at 35 per cent before it is paid to beneficiaries).

## THE SMALL SELF-ADMINISTERED SCHEME (SSAS)

The SSAS allows small companies to put large amounts into pension plans (usually for key employees or directors), without reference to the individual's own earnings or the limit on the annual amount they can pay into a plan. The contributions can be offset against the Corporation Tax the company would otherwise pay on its profits. The scheme can be used to build up a pension plan far more quickly than with normal employer contributions. However, HMRC can insist that payments in to the scheme are broadly in line with the real worth of an employee or director. This prevents firms shovelling fortunes into tax-free plans for those who would normally be low or average earners.

 For more about pensions, see the *Which? Essential Guides: Pension Handbook* and *Finance your Retirement*, or log on to www.which.co.uk/money. For further advice, seek also an independent financial adviser via the FSA website: www.unbiased.co.uk.

# Drawing your pension

While you're working, the only choices you need to make about personal or stakeholder pensions are how much to contribute and which investment fund or type to select. When you want to retire, you will have more choices, including when you want to draw your pension and, often, how much.

## WHEN CAN YOU CLAIM YOUR PENSION?

The minimum age at which you can take your state pension is 65 for a man and 60 for a woman born before 6 April 1950 rising in monthly increments to 65 for women born after 6 April 1955 (see page 16).

The minimum age for taking a private pension is now 55 – it used to be 50. At the same time, a number of concessions allowing primarily professional sports players to take their pension at an earlier age – as young as 35 in some cases – have been withdrawn.

You can draw your pension earlier in some cases – for example, because of serious ill health. In most cases, though, your pension will be reduced if you retire early. This is because you would normally be expected to draw it for a greater number of years. If your health is bad, you can apply for an enhanced annuity payment on the grounds you are unlikely to live longer than the average.

Your pension is counted as income for Income Tax purposes, no matter how old you are, but you cannot pay National Insurance on it.

If your employer's scheme allows it, you can draw part or all of your pension while continuing to work for your employer. In some cases, you will be able to contribute towards a second pension plan (but only a second and not any subsequent plans), providing you are under 75.

This may enable you to take the tax-free lump sum, which you can spend (see below), and continue to pay into a plan, thus potentially shielding your continuing earnings from tax. Check if this option is available with your employer's pension department.

## TAX-FREE CASH

In virtually all cases, you can take up to 25 per cent of any pension fund as tax-free cash, providing the scheme rules allow it – only a very few old (and generally very small) closed occupational schemes might not have this facility.

With a money purchase scheme, it's straightforward to work out the amount of cash you can take. It's 25 per cent of your total pension pot. It's more complex with a final salary employer plan (technically known as a defined benefit scheme), as it depends on the rate at which the scheme lets you exchange pension for cash. Your employer will give you the figures shortly before you retire.

You don't have to take the tax-free cash as this will reduce your pension in proportion – taking a 25 per cent lump sum would cut a £1,000 monthly pension to £750. But generally you should do. Even if you don't want to spend the money, it can be used as an investment to generate additional income but, unlike the pension you have, you have the flexibility to do what you like with your cash, including leaving it to your family in your will.

If the total of all your private pensions is worth 1 per cent or less of lifetime allowance, you can take the whole lot as cash. For the 2010–11 tax year, this means a limit of £18,000. Of this, 25 per cent can be taken tax free, the rest is taxed as income in the year you receive it. You must be aged between 60 and 75 to do this, and all pensions must be converted into cash in a one-year period.

## Buying an annuity

Once you have taken your 25 per cent tax-free lump sum, you must buy an annuity with what remains in a personal pension. But if you invest the lump sum in a further annuity, it will be taxed more lightly than exactly the same amount in the pension annuity bought with the remaining 75 per cent.

This is because there are two sorts of annuity. The compulsory purchase annuity is the device that turns the 75 per cent (or more from your pension fund or employer fund) into a regular income for the rest of your life (with the possibility of provision for your partner after your own death). Your income from this is taxed in exactly the same way as other income.

A non-compulsory annuity to provide a regular income for the rest of your life is known as a purchased life annuity. This is taxed at a special, less heavy rate, which takes into account that each payment from the annuity consists in part of the repayment of your own money. The formula is complicated and depends on your age – the older you are, the more generous it is – but you will be better off.

## OPTIONS FROM MONEY PURCHASE PENSIONS

There are many ways to get your pension pot out of money purchase schemes on retirement. But however you take your pension, it counts as taxable income. The most straightforward way of taking your pension is through an annuity, where you exchange capital for an income for life. You must do this when you reach the age of 75 – a rule that applies irrespective of your gender or when you actually retired. Most people choose to do this.

The annuity purchase is not popular with many due to its finality. There are some options that can provide an income up to the compulsory annuity age.

- **The lifetime annuity.** This option is only offered by one or two financial advice companies. Here you buy a fixed-term annuity, which lasts from the day of purchase until you reach 75. It then guarantees to give you the same lump sum that would have bought the same annuity as you had been receiving for the past years. But there is no guarantee that sum will buy the same income going forward – it may be more or less. Its advantage is a second bite at the cherry, which is especially useful if you have contracted a life-threatening illness that will shorten your life. It is also beneficial if you die before reaching 75 – your money will become part of your estate rather than being lost, as with a conventional annuity.

- **Income drawdown**, where you keep your pension fund invested but take an income from it. You can take income from your pension fund of between 0 and 120 per cent of the annuity income available. You could just take the tax-free lump sum. If you die while in drawdown, your dependants can inherit what's left in the fund. This can be paid as an annuity, as income from the fund, which is then taxed, or as a cash sum less 35 per cent tax.

By the age of 75 you have to take a pension from your employer (if available) or get an annuity. This annuity may be more or less than you might have received when you retired.

- **The Alternatively Secured Pension (ASP)** is a controversial idea, which could allow you to avoid the compulsory annuity purchase at age 75 by offering a continuing, if limited, form of income drawdown. When you die, any remaining ASP fund is used to provide a pension for any dependants (like a spouse). If there aren't any, it can theoretically be bequeathed to friends or family members' pension funds after IHT is paid at 40 per cent. In most schemes, the money is totally lost once you buy the annuity. The ASP is controversial because the Government said it was only set up to help those in religious groups, such as the Plymouth Brethren, who have a faith objection to annuities (which they see as a gamble on how long they have to live, which is unacceptable to them). However, many financial advisers saw IHT and other advantages for wealthy people by using the ASP. The Finance Act 2007 blocked these loopholes by creating a tax rate on 'unauthorised payment charges' (a way of attempting to pass on pension fund assets IHT-free) of up to 70 per cent. This renders it pointless as an avoidance measure.

> **" With income drawdown, you keep your pension fund invested but take an income from it between 0 and 120 per cent of the annuity income available. "**

## Pension questions on your tax return

If you get the main tax return (SA100), fill in question 11 if you get a UK pension from any source. As a result, you need details of the state pensions you were entitled to – either call Pensions Direct on 0845 301 3011 or get a BR735 form from your local Pensions Centre (see box, below). If you receive an employer's pension, or another type of private pension, you should get a P60.

For personal and stakeholder pensions, you need to enter the gross amount paid to all policies during 2009-10 in question 14. Don't include employer contributions or amounts you pay into employer-sponsored schemes.

Contributions are made net of basic-rate tax relief so you must add this back. You divide what you paid by 80 and multiply by 100. So, for example, if you pay £100, the grossed-up amount is £125.

You have to enter old-style retirement annuity contracts separately on to your tax return.

To find your local pensions centre, go to www.thepensionservice.gov.uk/contactus/home.asp or you can phone the Pension Service on 0845 60 60 265 (8am-8pm, Monday-Friday).

**115**

# Other retirement savings

Pensions offer a powerful set of tax advantages including tax relief on payments made into a scheme, and a substantial degree of tax freedom for the investments the scheme makes. And there is a tax-free lump sum at the end when you draw your pension on retirement.

Pensions nevertheless have drawbacks in return for the tax help. Once you have paid your money in, you cannot have it back (except when you leave a company scheme in the first two years of membership), even if you have an overwhelming need for cash. And when you reach 75, you have to turn the plan (less any tax-free lump sum) into an annuity, which is taxed as income.

You can, of course, save for your retirement in any way that you wish, including direct investment into the stock market or buy-to-let properties. But the main alternative that is attractive from a tax point of view is the Individual Savings Account – the ISA.

Everyone aged 18 or over can invest up to £10,200 a year into a variety of funds, investment trusts or, more rarely, individual shares. You can also invest part of your fund into cash but not into direct property purchases. The £10,200 is due to rise with inflation each year.

Their big (and for many, over-riding) drawback over pensions is that you do not get tax relief on payments on the way in, so you may not be able to afford to invest so much. But like pensions, they grow in a tax-favoured environment with no Income Tax or CGT to worry about.

Unlike pensions, you can cash them in when and how you want. You don't have to wait for a retirement age if you need the money before then. Equally, you can keep them as long as you like – there is no insistence that you buy an annuity before you reach 75.

You can withdraw the tax-free income to help fund your retirement as and how you like – there is no need for complicated vehicles such as drawdown funds. And that may be helpful for the many whose funds are not large enough to warrant the expense and hassles of such a fund (see pages 118–21).

**❝The main alternative to a pension for making savings is the ISA, which is attractive from a tax point of view.❞**

# Savings and investments

Your savings and investments are subject to two taxes – Income Tax and Capital Gains Tax (CGT). You may be liable to pay one or the other – or perhaps both. This chapter deals with investments and Income Tax that you will generally pay on an annual basis. The following chapter looks at CGT, which you only need to consider if and when you dispose of certain investments or other assets.

# Tax-free options

It may seem tough that as well as having to pay tax on the money we earn, we may also have to pay more tax on income we receive from our savings and investments. However, there are many investments with tax advantages. Wherever possible – and always taking account of investment and savings conditions first – these tax breaks should form the building blocks for money we put away to grow for later on.

## INDIVIDUAL SAVINGS ACCOUNTS (ISAs)

ISAs are totally free of Income Tax and, where it might apply, CGT. The annual limit is £10,200. Up to £5,100 of this can go into a cash ISA – the balance is available to invest in stocks and shares. These limits will be increased each year in line with inflation.

## Cash ISAs

Anyone aged 16 or over can take out a cash ISA – they're sold by most banks and building societies and by National Savings & Investments. But those aged 16 or 17 can only use money that is theirs from sources other than their parents, such as earnings from employment or cash from other family members such as grandparents as income arising from a parental ISA gift contributes to the £100 income limit.

You can invest up to £5,100 each tax year, either as a lump sum or in regular or irregular instalments, although some plans limit how you can pay. Your money will generally go into a savings account, which will earn interest either at a fixed rate for a set period or on a variable basis.

Some also offer stock market-based savings. These are for a set period – typically five to six years – and promise

### Tax freedom can be valuable

It is always worthwhile making a tax-free investment – always assuming the terms and conditions are at least as good as the comparable taxed investments. The most basic tax-free investment is the cash ISA (Individual Savings Account) from banks and building societies. It may often be better than the equivalent taxed account. Someone earning 3 per cent from a £10,000 cash tax-free ISA account ends up with £300 a year in interest.

The same person earning the same amount on the same sum would end up with £240 (2.4 per cent) if they were a basic-rate taxpayer or £180 (1.8 per cent) if a 40 per cent taxpayer. The interest payable after tax to top-rate taxpayers is now roughly in line with inflation - their money has to run fast to stand still in spending cash terms.

a return based on stock market performance at the end of the product's life rather than a regular income. To qualify as a cash ISA, they must give you back at least the money you put in, irrespective of share price levels.

You can build up ISAs year on year – moving money from taxed accounts if you wish – but each year's payment can be with a different savings institution. You can also move ISAs around from bank to bank.

Interest payments that you leave in ISAs; instead of withdrawing them, they continue to grow tax free. But you can never replace cash into your ISA account once you have withdrawn it – even in the same tax year. You can only have one cash ISA with one savings firm in a tax year. All ISAs are sold on a use-it or lose-it basis, so if you miss out on the concession for a year, you have abandoned it forever. Additionally, ISAs do not have to be reported on self-assessment tax forms – an extra bonus!

> **"Cash ISAs offering stock market-based savings last for a set period and promise a return based on stock market performance."**

## Ask the expert

### I do not pay tax – should I get an ISA?

Yes. Although you can reclaim tax (see page 123) on bank and building society interest, you may not always be in this position. For instance, you may be a student who will eventually get full-time paid employment or someone taking a career break or having family responsibilities. In these cases, you will probably be a taxpayer in the future but your ISA will always stay outside the tax net. The ISA is also easier than claiming the tax back on an individual basis.

## Whatever happened to personal equity plans?

Personal equity plans (PEPs) ceased being available in 1999. To all intents and purposes, from the private investor point of view, they are now interchangeable with ISAs and are treated in the same way as an ISA.

**119**

## Jargon buster

**Bonds** These allow governments, international bodies and companies to borrow, usually for a fixed time at a fixed annual interest rate. They are traded on the stock market so their value can go up and down

**Corporate bonds** Bonds from companies in the UK and elsewhere. They often pay a higher rate of return compared to bonds from governments

**Enterprise Investment Scheme (EIS)** A government-approved scheme offering tax relief to investors in small, and often risky, companies, not quoted on the stock market

**Film finance plans** A number of complex schemes aimed at the very wealthy, which offer tax benefits to those backing UK film productions

**Gilts** (or gilt-edged securities) Government bonds that pay a fixed rate of interest, usually for a fixed time limit

**Investment trust** A company whose sole purpose is to invest in a basket of shares from other companies

**Shares** (also known as equities) These give holders the right to dividends and a say in the company's running – in proportion to the amount of shares held. Many shares are traded on the stock market and can rise or fall

**Unit trust (or an open-ended investment company (OEIC))** An investment in a basket of shares so where investors can spread their equity-owning risks

**Venture Capital Trust (VCT)** Allows investors to spread risks across a basket of small and start-up company shares with tax relief

 You can now transfer any unused cash ISA allowance into a stocks and shares ISA, but not the other way around. For example, if you put £1,000 into a cash ISA, you can invest up to £9,200 (the £10,200 maximum less the £1,000 cash) into stocks and shares.

## Stocks and shares ISAs

Provided you are 18 or over, you can invest up to £10,200 into stocks and shares. Permitted investments into stocks and shares ISAs include unit trusts, investment trusts, individual shares, corporate bonds and British government loan stocks (known as 'gilts').

Provided you don't go over the limit, you can pay a lump sum or regularly or irregularly – depending on the rules of your preferred investment. Some only allow one investment a year or penalise those putting in less than the maximum with higher charges.

You can only have one ISA in a tax year. But ISA wrapper products from online investment supermarkets allow you to put funds from several management firms into the one ISA account if you wish. ISAs can be moved around so you are not stuck with one dud fund manager forever.

## OTHER TAX-SAVING INVESTMENTS

Venture Capital Trusts (VCTs), Enterprise Investment Schemes (EISs) and some film finance plans all offer various forms of tax relief in exchange for putting your money into higher-risk investments. A VCT – a form of investment trust that puts your money into a portfolio of unquoted companies – gives Income Tax relief on your investment money provided you hold on for five years, while an EIS investment gives Income Tax relief and allows you to put off paying CGT bills accrued elsewhere. These vehicles are complex, however, and the tax saved may be wiped out because

## Ask the expert

### What are the tax benefits of stocks and shares ISAs?

There is no Income Tax to pay on stocks and shares ISAs, but how much you save depends on your personal tax position and the investment you buy.

Basic taxpayers no longer enjoy any advantages on share dividend taxation. They pay the same rate whether the investment is in an ISA or not, so there is no benefit here. They do not lose out by this, however, and, indeed, would gain if their earnings rise so they become 40 per cent taxpayers.

Higher-rate taxpayers would normally have to pay an additional 22.5 per cent tax rate on their share dividends via self-assessment tax forms, those on the 50 per cent rate, a further 32.5 per cent. There is nothing to pay if the investment is sheltered in an ISA.

There is no CGT to pay when an investment is sold at a profit although loss-making investments cannot be offset against a CGT bill arising outside of an ISA.

The benefits of investing in corporate or government bond funds are different. These are treated for tax purposes as if they produced savings account interest (see opposite). Funds that consist of both bonds and shares are treated as if they were bond funds provided the bond element is 60 per cent or more. Not all bond funds are liable for capital gains tax.

many of these schemes lose investors' money. The film plans are usually highly risky and aimed at those with substantial fortunes. You should never invest in any of these without taking independent advice.

## NATIONAL SAVINGS & INVESTMENTS (NS&I)

National Savings & Investments (NS&I) offers several tax-free products, including cash ISAs, savings certificates (fixed-interest and index-linked) and children's bonus bonds. These offer the biggest advantages to top-rate taxpayers. A 3 per cent annual tax-free return is the same as 3.75 per cent in a taxable account for a basic-rate taxpayer, 5 per cent to a 40 per cent taxpayer or 6 per cent to a 50 per cent taxpayer.

Winnings on premium bonds where the chance of big lump sum prizes is substituted for interest payments are also tax free.

**“ NS&I products offer the biggest advantages to top-rate taxpayers. ”**

## CHILD TRUST FUNDS (CTFs)

Parents of children born from 1 September 2002 receive at least £250 (it's £500 for children of lower income parents) for investment into a child trust

121

fund (CTF) when the parent starts receiving Child Benefit. Parents receive a further payment when the child reaches seven. The fund money can be invested in cash or stocks and shares – just like an ISA – and all the proceeds are free of Income Tax and any CGT.

For most children, savings that are designated as theirs will be tax free anyway – few children earn enough to pay tax. But the advantage of the CTF for those who can afford it is that a further £1,200 a year can be added to the fund for the child's behalf. This money can come from friends and family – including parents who are normally severely restricted in the amounts they can give their children without the income being counted as part of their own tax bill.

## FRIENDLY SOCIETIES

Friendly societies offer investments through insurance plans that are tax free to the purchaser. The policies, which can cover a variety of investments, must have a life of at least ten years. Many are designed to last until a child reaches 18 or 21. But charges can be high, especially in the early years, wiping out many (and sometimes all or even more than all) of the benefits of their tax-free status. You can invest up to £270 a year, if paid in a lump sum, or £300 a year if paid monthly.

**❝ Friendly society charges can be high in the early years. ❞**

---

## Quick tax-saving tips

- Cash ISAs often pay better rates that most ordinary saving accounts and the interest is tax free, so they should be your first home for any spare cash savings.
- Couples may be able to save tax by transferring savings or investments to the partner that pays the least tax - especially if one is a higher-rate taxpayer and one is a non-taxpayer (see pages 87-8 for more details).
- Non-taxpayers should complete form R85 (see page 92) so interest on bank and building society accounts can be paid gross (see opposite). And don't forget to do this for children as well (see pages 92-8 for more details of tax and children).

## Jargon buster

Friendly society Life insurance company that is allowed to issue tax-free investment plans. The friendly society label can be confusing. Most friendly societies also sell standard insurance policies that are not tax free

---

 For more information on Child Trust Funds, see pages 93-4. See also the website www.childtrustfund.gov.uk, which explains how you can open, contribute to and manage an account.

# Taxed options

Despite the fact that we may have to pay tax on our savings, it's not all doom and gloom. You may be able to reclaim all or some of the tax deducted if your income is low. Savings income is effectively taxed more lightly than your salary if you are under state retirement age because there is no National Insurance to pay.

This section looks at savings and investments where some tax is deducted by the financial institution. The majority of investments fit into this category. There are three main forms of taxation – on interest, on dividends and on investment-based life insurance policies and bonds.

## TAX ON SAVINGS INCOME

Interest on taxed savings like bank or building society accounts is paid after tax of 20 per cent has been deducted by the financial institution, which pays it directly to HMRC on your behalf. Basic-rate Income Taxpayers have no more to pay and do not need to declare this income in most circumstances.

There is no National Insurance to pay either, so tax from savings is at 20 per cent while tax from income for basic-rate payers under retirement age works out at 31 per cent.

But higher-rate taxpayers have to pay a further 20 per cent, usually using the self-assessment tax return. Added to the 20 per cent already taken, it brings the tax on their savings income up to the 40 per cent top rate. If you don't receive

## Claiming tax back

If you know that your gross savings income – the amount before any tax is deducted – plus any other earnings you have will be within your Personal Allowance, then ensure you sign form R85 at your bank or building society. The savings firm will normally have its own pre-printed forms.

You need only fill one form R85 as it goes from year to year (assuming your circumstances do not change), but you will normally have to complete a new form every time you open another account – even with the same bank or building society. Form R85 allows you to be paid without any tax being taken off. If you discover later on that your income is higher, then you must tell the tax inspector and repay the tax.

This is most easily done with form R40 'Claim for Repayment' – available from the HMRC. Form R40 can also be used by non-taxpayers (those earning less than the Personal Allowance) who did not claim through form R85 'Getting your interest without tax taken off'.

If you have no or low earnings from employment or pensions and rely on savings interest, you may find part of your interest is taxed at 20 per cent, some at 10 per cent (the first £2,440 above your Personal Allowance) and some at 0 per cent.

&&There is no National Insurance to pay on savings income. **

a tax return and you have income from savings that might fall into the top tax rate, it's your responsibility to tell your Income Tax office about it.

## DIVIDEND INCOME

This type of income is paid with a 10 per cent Tax Credit, regardless of whether you choose to reinvest your income or have the dividend paid in cash (or in new shares through dividend reinvestment plans). This means, in effect, that 10 per cent tax has already been deducted from your dividend before you receive it.

Basic-rate taxpayers have no further tax to pay. Non-taxpayers also have this tax deducted, but unlike savings income, can't claim it back. Higher-rate taxpayers pay a further 22.5 per cent (of the gross dividend), again usually by completing a tax return and paying through the self-assessment route.

## HOW MUCH DO YOU PAY?

As with most tax questions, the answer is – it all depends! The variables include the type of savings or investments you have and how much other income you possess. As a general rule, nearly all investments are paid 'net of basic-rate

Basic-rate taxpayers with incomes from earnings at or approaching the higher-rate threshold (£43,875, 2010-11) will have to take care. If their total income, including the savings income, exceeds the threshold, they will be liable for higher-rate tax on the amount above this threshold.

tax' – the basic-rate taxpayer does not have to do anything more as the deductions are made at source. Top-rate taxpayers will have to pay more – through their self-assessment form.

## WHAT TYPE OF INCOME IS IT?

The income that comes from savings or investments that produce interest (as opposed to dividends) is usually known as savings income. Whether the savings income is paid once, twice or more often a year, and whether you leave it to grow or take it out and spend it, HMRC is interested in how much each account earns every year. Investments that produce interest that is generally taxable include:

- Bank or building society accounts.
- National Savings & Investments (except non-taxable products such as savings certificates or premium bonds).

**‟ Nearly all investments are paid 'net of basic rate tax' - deductions for the basic-rate taxpayer are made at source, top-rate taxpayers have to pay more. ”**

- Permanent income-bearing shares (PIBS) from building societies.
- Gilts.
- Corporate bonds.
- Local authority fixed-interest investments.
- Unit trusts or open-ended investment companies (OEICs), which invest mainly in money funds in order to produce interest.

## Dividend income

This comes from shares you own in companies (as well as from unit trusts, investment trusts and OEICs) that invest mainly in shares. Not all shares or all unit or investment trusts pay dividends.

Life insurance investments, including with-profit bonds, can also be used to provide a regular investment income, but these are taxed in a special way, both in the hands of the insurance company and in the hands of the policy owner.

**“HMRC like to know about the income that comes from savings or investments producing interest. ”**

## Tax rates on investment income

There are two distinct sets of tax rates. One is for savings income, and the second for dividend income.

- Tax on interest payments from savings is paid at 0, 10, 20, 40 or 50 per cent, depending on what other income you have. Non-taxpayers may be able to reclaim some or all of the basic-rate tax, which is deducted by the savings institution at source (see page 123). Top-rate taxpayers, however, have to pay more – usually through their self-assessment form.

- Tax on dividend income is effectively paid at 10, 32.5 or 42.5 per cent. Basic taxpayers do not have to pay anything more. Higher and additional-rate payers have to pay more, but those paying no tax cannot reclaim any tax.

## What do I do with foreign shares?

Paying the right tax on dividends received from overseas companies can be complex – whether paid in sterling or in a foreign currency (when you will need to make an exchange calculation based on the amount of sterling you eventually banked). You may also have to work out foreign withholding tax, double taxation agreements and other complications – it can all depend on which country sent you the dividend cheque.

These dividends should be reported on the foreign income supplementary pages of the self-assessment form – SA106. This comes complete with 28 pages of notes including the different rates needed for countries from Antigua to Zimbabwe.

But, in most cases, the effect of all these calculations is generally a matter of a few pounds difference from the amount investors would pay if it is was a UK dividend – only a very few taxpayers have significantly large foreign dividend payments. Some are so small that the costs of converting the cheque into sterling are greater than its value.

So HMRC decided to be practical and pragmatic – spurred on by the takeover of Abbey National by Spanish-owned Banco Santander. This put many hundreds of thousands who would otherwise have had no need to complete a tax return into the self-assessment group. The cost of processing all these forms would have been substantially above any extra tax collected.

As a result, HMRC has decided effectively to ignore foreign income dividends up to an annual value of £300 for those who would otherwise have not filled in a return, or have the short tax return (see page 183). They are treated as though they arose in the UK – so basic-rate taxpayers need do nothing and pay nothing more. This applies to all foreign shares – not just those issued by Banco Santander.

Those people who file online or use one of the HMRC-approved software packages will find the sums are calculated automatically.

## HOW MUCH WILL YOU HAVE TO PAY?

To find out what rate you'll pay follow these steps:

**Step 1:** Add your savings and investment income to any other income you have. This will be on your P60 (P45 for job leavers) if you are in employment or it is the profit as stated on your accounts if you are self-employed.

**Step 2:** Deduct your Personal Allowance (see pages 10–11) together with any other tax reliefs you might be entitled to.

**Step 3:** If the level of these allowances exceeds your total income, then you will not pay any tax and may be able to reclaim savings interest tax taken by the bank or building society. You will not have any extra to pay on dividend income.

**Step 4:** If any remaining income falls within the 10 per cent starting-rate band, then you'll pay 10 per cent on savings income – you should be able to reclaim the savings tax deducted at source. You will not have to pay anything on investment income from shares.

**Step 5:** If any savings or dividend income falls into the basic-rate tax band (£2,440–£37,400 for 2010–11), but

with a higher starting level for some older people (see pages 10–11), in theory you'll pay 20 per cent on the savings income and 10 per cent on the dividend income. But in practice, as most savings products deduct interest at the basic rate and all shares automatically arrive with the 10 per cent already paid, there will be nothing more to account for.

**Step 6:** Whatever is left falls into the higher-rate tax bands. This starts with a total income of £43,875 (2010–11). Here you'll pay 40 or 50 per cent on the savings income and 32.5 or 42.5 per cent on dividend income – less any tax taken and credited.

## The rates you really pay at a glance

| If your taxable income for 2010-11 is ... | On savings income you pay ... | On dividend income you pay ... |
| --- | --- | --- |
| Up to £6,475 | Nothing but you may be able to reclaim tax | Nothing - the 10% tax has already been deducted |
| £6,475 to £8,915 (on savings income) | 10% tax on any income in this band (but you must first count income from work) [1] | Nothing, but you cannot reclaim anything |
| £6,475 to £37,400 | 20% tax on any income that falls in this band less what has already been deducted, so nothing on most savings plans | 10% tax on any income that falls in this band less what has already been deducted, leaving nothing more to pay |
| £37,400 to £150,000 | 40% tax on any income that falls in this band less what has already been deducted | 32.5% tax on any income that falls in this band less what has already been deducted, leaving a 22.5% tax bill |
| Over £150,000 | 50% tax on any income that falls in this band less what has already been deducted | 42.5% tax on any income that falls in this band less what has already been deducted, leaving a 32.5% tax bill |

[1] You may be able to reclaim the difference between this 10% and the 20% deducted at source

# Investments where no tax is taken

A minority of investments pay income without a tax deduction (known as paid gross), but this doesn't mean tax isn't due. These are often known as 'taxable investments and savings'. Unless you are a non-taxpayer, you have to declare what you earn on them and pay the tax due.

## National Savings & Investments (NS&I)

Interest payments on capital bonds, income bonds, guaranteed equity bonds, investment accounts, pensioners' bonds and the easy access savings account (EASA) are all paid gross.

## Gilts (British government stocks)

The dividend (often known technically as the 'coupon') on gilts bought since 6 April 1998 is usually paid gross, but you can ask to have it paid with tax already deducted. Conversely, interest on gilts bought before 6 April 1998 is usually paid with tax deducted, but you can choose to be paid gross.

## Corporate bonds and permanent interest-bearing shares

If you invest directly into corporate bonds and permanent interest-bearing shares (PIBS), most will pay the interest gross, so you will have to declare it on your tax return if there is tax to pay. But if you invest into corporate bonds via a unit trust, your dividends will be paid less the basic 20 per cent rate tax, so you will only have to act if you can reclaim tax as a zero payer or have to pay more as a top 40 per cent payer.

## Offshore accounts

Interest on offshore accounts and investment funds, such as those based in the Channel Islands or the Isle of Man, is paid gross, unlike similar accounts onshore. But this doesn't mean it's tax free. UK residents are normally charged on the full amount of foreign income arising abroad, whether it is brought into the UK or not. You need to declare this type of income on your tax return using special supplementary pages for foreign income.

## OFFSHORE ACCOUNTS

Using an offshore account is legal but attempting to evade tax by not declaring your income is illegal. Since a court ruling in early 2006, HMRC has the power to oblige banks and other offshore institutions with UK businesses to disclose details of account holders who may be resident in the UK. It would not be able to force this legal point on banks that are totally outside the UK jurisdiction – such as a Kazakhstan bank set up in Vanuatu (at least one does exist) – but the tax authorities would be able to ask the provenance of large sums of money that suddenly appear or for you to explain where you got the money for substantial assets that you have recently purchased.

Some countries may also make a tax charge on your savings, irrespective of whether you are paying UK tax or not. If this happens to you, make sure you declare this as well, as you can usually claim a UK Tax Credit for any tax charged on your savings by another country under 'double taxation agreements'. HMRC is increasingly discovering previously 'hidden' accounts. From time to time, it offers an amnesty allowing account holders to own up to their evasion.

## LIFE INSURANCE AND SINGLE PREMIUM BONDS

If you think of life insurance as an insurance policy that pays out when you die or are diagnosed with a critical illness, you would be right. But many life policies combine cover with investment, with some offering virtually no life cover at all beyond the value of the policy plus a tiny

percentage. These investments are designed to take advantage of often esoteric life insurance tax rules.

The most common types of life insurance investment policies are endowments, unit-linked policies and single-premium investment bonds, usually with profits bonds. There are two types of policy – qualifying and non-qualifying.

## Qualifying policies

To count as a qualifying policy, a life insurance has to have regular premiums, which must run for at least ten years or

*Continued on page 132*

> ❝ Life insurance investment policies include endowments, unit-linked policies and single-premium investment bonds. ❞

Many financial advisers, who can earn high commissions on insurance-based investments, try to suggest these policies are 'tax free'. What they may mean is that the holder has no further tax to pay because tax has already been taken from the insurance company itself. Life companies pay a special composite tax rate instead of the Income Tax and CGT other investors would normally pay. Individuals cannot reclaim this tax; many would be better off with other forms of investment, such as unit and investment trusts.

**129**

# How investments are taxed

Our table shows how some investments are taxed for UK residents.

**Taxable** means you have tax to pay (unless you are a non-taxpayer)

**Taxed** means tax has already been deducted

**Tax free** is self-explanatory

| Type of income | Status | | | Notes |
|---|---|---|---|---|
| | Taxable | Taxed | Tax free | |
| Accounts (held in £ or foreign currency) at a UK branch of a bank or building society | | ✓ | | Non-taxpayers can receive this gross |
| Accounts at an offshore (e.g. Jersey, Isle of Man) branch of a UK or foreign bank or building society | ✓ | | | |
| Annuities | | ✓ | | Non-taxpayers can receive this gross |
| British government stocks (gilts) acquired since 6 April 1998 | ✓ | | | No CGT to pay: taxpayers can apply for net payment |
| British government stocks (other) | | ✓ | | No CGT to pay: taxpayers can apply to receive gross |
| Child trust funds | | | ✓ | But dividends taxed at 10%, which can't be reclaimed |
| Co-operative Society deposits | ✓ | | | |
| Corporate bonds, debentures, loan stock and other fixed-income investments | ✓ | | | No CGT if they count as qualifying corporate bonds |
| Credit union deposits | ✓ | | | |
| Friendly society tax-exempt plans | | | ✓ | But dividends taxed at 10%, which can't be reclaimed |
| Interest from private individuals | ✓ | | | |
| Interest on distributions under a will | | ✓ | | |
| Cash ISAs | | | ✓ | |
| Stocks and shares ISAs | | | ✓ | But dividends taxed at 10%, which can't be reclaimed |
| Loans to foreign governments | | ✓ | | In foreign currency, may be received gross but taxable |
| Local authority loans | | ✓ | | Non-taxpayers can receive this gross |

| Type of income | Status | | | Notes |
|---|---|---|---|---|
| | Taxable | Taxed | Tax free | |
| NS&I: easy access savings account (EASA) | ✓ | | | |
| National Savings Certificates | | | ✓ | |
| National Savings children's bonus bonds | | | ✓ | |
| National Savings fixed-rate savings bonds | ✓ | | | |
| National Savings: other accounts and bonds | ✓ | | | |
| Offshore managed funds | ✓ | | | |
| Open-ended investment company distributions (OEICS) | | ✓ | | Profits on sale taxed as capital gains |
| Permanent interest-bearing shares (PIBS) | ✓ | | | No CGT if counted as qualifying corporate bonds |
| Personal equity plans (PEPs) | | | ✓ | But dividends taxed at 10%, which cannot be reclaimed |
| Premium bond prizes | | | ✓ | |
| Proceeds from non-qualifying UK life insurance policies | ✓ | | | Only if you pay higher-rate tax; if not, treated as a qualifying policy (below) |
| Proceeds from qualifying UK life insurance policies (usually) | | | ✓ | But insurance company has paid tax, which can't be reclaimed |
| Proceeds from non-UK life insurance policies | ✓ | | | |
| Save-as-you-earn accounts (SAYE) | | | ✓ | |
| Share dividends from UK companies | | ✓ | | Profits on sale taxed as capital gains |
| Tax rebate interest | | | ✓ | |
| Traded options | | ✓ | | Taxed as capital gains unless linked to gilts or qualifying corporate bonds |
| Trusts and settlements: income payments to beneficiaries | | ✓ | | |
| Unit trust distributions | | ✓ | | Profits on sale taxed as capital gains |
| War loan | ✓ | | | No CGT to pay |

for at least 75 per cent of its term if this amounts to less than ten years. So seven-and-a-half years is the absolute minimum. Most regular savings endowments or unit-linked policies or other investment-based monthly or annual payment insurance plans are designed as qualifying plans.

The advantage of a qualifying investment is that there is no further tax to pay beyond that which the insurance company has paid in its special composite rate. This is advantageous for top-rate taxpayers as the composite rate is substantially below 40 per cent; broadly neutral for basic-rate taxpayers, but not helpful to non-taxpayers who cannot reclaim the tax paid by the insurer.

Holders of qualifying policies do not have to declare maturity or surrender proceeds on their tax forms.

## Non-qualifying policies

Any other insurance-based investment is non-qualifying. In general, this normally means single premium or lump sum investments that go into a bond – a policy that can still benefit some people by using the life insurance taxation rules. You can usually recognise these because there is only a minimal level of life cover – typically the value of the fund plus 1 per cent, so they offer no real protection whatsoever.

The taxation of non-qualifying policies is complex. There are special rules on how much you can take out each year as income without paying tax that year. In general, this is 5 per cent of the original investment. If the holder pays basic rate tax at the time of encashment, there is no more tax to pay.

## ARE THERE OTHER INVESTMENT TAXES?

Purchasers of most shares, including investment trusts, have to pay 0.5 per cent stamp duty when they buy. There is no way around this and it is impossible to reclaim. Unit trusts (OIECs) also have this charge but it is built in to the fee structure so it is not shown separately. But some stock market purchases do not attract stamp duty. These include:

- Shares sold through initial public offerings (IPOs) – also known as flotations.
- Government and corporate bonds.
- Contracts for difference.
- Traded options.
- Warrants.
- Spread bets.
- Exchange traded funds.
- Other derivative-based (futures and options) investments.

Other than IPOs and bonds, most of the investments are designed for frequent or professional investors who would most notice the effect of paying 0.5 per cent every time they switch an investment.

"Purchasers of most shares, including investment trusts, have to pay 0.5 per cent stamp duty when they buy."

# Tax on assets

This chapter focuses on Capital Gains Tax (CGT) – the tax you may pay when you sell something at a profit. This is a tax on the money you make from successful investment and other asset sales. A couple could, however, potentially save almost £2,000 a year thanks to a use-it or lose-it tax relief.

# Capital gains

Capital Gains Tax is charged when you dispose of certain investments and assets for more than you paid for them. But many investments and assets are outside this tax net - the home you live in is generally the most important.

## ASSETS THAT ESCAPE CAPITAL GAINS TAX

The good news is that many assets always escape CGT when you sell them. The term 'selling' can include swapping assets with a party other than your spouse or civil partner, giving items away, or – in extreme cases to prevent tax evasion – when an asset is destroyed without being replaced or where there is no successful insurance claim.

You are most likely to pay the tax if you are an active investor buying and selling, say, shares and unit trusts or you sell or give away a large asset, such as a second home or a business. However, many other items are outside this tax's orbit.

- **Your main residence.** This is the property that you consider to be your primary home. You can generally only have one at any one time (in the tax inspector's eyes) – no matter how complicated your personal life might be. The exceptions to this rule are considered fully on pages 164–5.
- **Personal assets** (legally known as chattels), which are sold for less than £6,000. This would include items of daily use such as furniture, clothing, bicycles, computers (used personally rather than in a business), and other home electrical and electronic items.
- **'Wasting assets'.** This takes in anything with a projected life of under 50 years, including caravans and boats. It would include a cellar of white wine but not one of port – white wine has a relatively short shelf life while vintage port can be drinkable for well over 100 years. The wasting asset definition may also include some works of art that are designed to physically disintegrate within that period – animals pickled in formaldehyde for example.
- **Tax-advantaged investment schemes,** including ISAs (as of 2008–9 this includes the predecessor personal equity plans (PEPs)) and the final bonus from Save As You Earn schemes (SAYE) (but

 You cannot offset losses in tax-advantaged investments, such as ISAs, against CGT payable elsewhere.

not the proceeds of shares from SAYE schemes if you eventually sell them on at a profit).

- **Shares in Venture Capital Trusts** and Enterprise Investment Schemes, provided you hold your investment for a minimum period (see pages 120–1).
- **British government bonds,** often known as 'gilts' – and most sterling-based corporate bonds. This includes permanent interest-bearing shares (PIBS) from building societies.
- **National Savings & Investments.** Anything from its range, including stock market-based investments.
- **Savings accounts** – these are taxed as income.
- **Gains on investment-based life insurance policies.** The insurance company pays tax at a special rate before calculating what you have earned, so you have no liability.
- **Payments from protection-style policies,** such as critical illness plans (which give a lump sum if you are diagnosed with certain medical conditions).
- **Compensation** awarded by a court following an injury or defamation claim.
- **Private cars and motorcycles.** These can be of any value but they must be vehicles you have used (or, in some circumstances, intended to use). Vintage and classic vehicles are the most likely assets to fit this category.
- **Gains from gambling,** including such things as horse racing, casino games, lotteries, football pools and bingo. This heading also takes in 'spread betting', which can be used as an investment alternative to shares, but if you spread

 If you frequently buy and sell cars, HMRC will consider you are trading and tax you as a business. Those who pay a deposit on a new car (perhaps one with a limited production run or where there is a waiting list) with the intention of selling it unused at a profit will be liable either to CGT or to be taxed as a trader. The new CGT rate is lower at 18 per cent than Income Tax. But traders may be able to offset more expenses against their profits if they are assessed under Income Tax.

## Tax tip

Most chattels decline in value. But if you do have something to sell that has increased in value and is worth more than £6,000, you may be able to break the sale into two or more parts – a table and chairs for instance. There is a special rule that can be used when the price received is a little over £6,000. This 'five-thirds' (1.6666) rule means tax can be limited to the amount over £6,000 multiplied by 5/3. It means chattels have their own built-in allowance irrespective of what was paid for them or whether you have used up your annual allowance elsewhere. See HMRC helpsheet IR293 'Chattels and CGT' for the current tax year.

bet as your main source of income you will be liable for income tax.

- **British currency,** including sovereigns dated from 1837 (the start of Queen Victoria's reign). Older sovereign coins are classed as antiques. This rule does not apply to non-British gold coins such as kruggerrands.
- **Foreign currency,** but only if you have bought it for reasonable personal use. This would include holiday money and cash used to maintain a home

overseas (but not the cash for a potential purchase). This definition would only start to concern you if you managed to sell the currency back to the bank or travel agent at a profit.

- **Decorations for bravery,** but only if you won them yourself. Otherwise, they count as antiques.

## ASSETS POSSIBLY LIABLE FOR CAPITAL GAINS TAX

Many items that can be bought and then sold at a profit count for CGT. Among the most frequent are:

- **Shares.** This includes investment trusts and most unit trusts. You could also pay the tax on a number of equity derivative schemes, such as exchange traded funds or contracts for difference where you invest in an asset without legally owning it.
- **Foreign currency options.** These are 'bets' against a currency rising or falling. This includes a wide variety of futures and options as well as physically holding the money but not spread betting on currency moves.
- **Antiques and works of art.** This could include valuable furniture and items such as rare books and records.

---

### Tax tip

Gifts of shares and other assets to registered charities and certain other good causes, including museums and community sports clubs, do not attract CGT. It may be worth donating items that have a substantial CGT liability rather than those that do not. In that way you save more tax while still showing the good cause the same amount of generosity.

---

*"* Many items that can be bought and sold at a profit, such as shares and antiques, count for CGT. *"*

---

Shares that you have acquired for nothing, such as those offered in building society and insurance company demutualisations, are also potentially taxable when you sell them with HMRC working out the profit from what you paid for them. If the purchase price was zero, then the tax could be payable on the entire amount you receive.

- **The value of a business.** Whether it's entirely your own business or you share it with others or it's simply considered a 'business asset', you may have a tax liability if you sell at a profit.
- **Second homes.** In general, selling any home or property other than the one that is considered your 'main residence' for more than you paid for it gives rise to a possible capital gains bill. It does not matter whether you live in your second home or lend it to friends or sometimes let it out to others.
- **Buy-to-let properties.** These are treated identically to second homes – see pages 176–80 for more details.
- **Anything else that's not in the tax-free list.** The list of assets that are excluded from CGT (see pages 134–6) is a good check. If you cannot find what you are selling in it, then assume it is potentially taxable. That way, you cannot get into problems for not declaring an asset sale to HMRC. No list can be totally exhaustive and there are 'grey areas' in fields as distinct as wine, art and investment bonds. HMRC will tell you if an item is taxable – but if you are still doubtful, this advice can be legally challenged.

## HOW MUCH TAX WILL I HAVE TO PAY?

CGT is a 'voluntary tax' as it is up to you to inform HMRC, but you only rack up a potential liability when you sell assets that fall into its net profitably. Everyone has an allowance. In 2010–11, the first £10,100 of gains comes tax free. But this is a use-it or lose-it free slice, which most people fail to make the most of.

> **❝ If you can't find what you are selling in the list of assets that escape CGT, then assume it is potentially taxable. It is best to err on the side of caution. ❞**

## Running your own business

If you run your own business and sell up, you could qualify for a special low 10 per cent CGT rate. Under new rules, business owners can pay at this level rather than the standard 18 per cent for the first £1 million of such gains in their lifetime. This saves up to £80,000 over the years.

To qualify as a business owner, you must have at least 5 per cent of the company's shares or be a sole trader (where you will own 100 per cent of the company's shares) or be a partner with at least a 5 per cent degree of control and profit taking.

**137**

## Children and Capital Gains Tax

Parents who give money to their children are usually severely restricted as they can only invest limited amounts into bank and building society accounts on their children's behalf. Money given in this way cannot attract interest of more than £100 per parent so, in practical terms at current interest rates, the sum that each parent can give each child before there is a tax bill on the parent is limited to around £2,000.

But this rule only applies when there is an income. Many shares and collective investments (unit and investment trusts) do not produce any income at all or, if they do, it is so small that it falls below the £100 level. With such non-income producing assets, parents can give their offspring limitless amounts. But providing there are gains, the parent who holds the child's assets through a simple

trust mechanism (unit and investment trust managers will help with this) can cash in up to the annual allowance (£10,100 in 2010-11) without paying any tax at all.

If the sums involved were large enough and the assets grew sufficiently, such a trust could give each child nearly £10,000 a year in tax-free income. A parent could pay nearly £4,000 in Income Tax if the same money came from interest earned rather than capital growth.

The downside of this is risk. While interest will always mean your money increases, and you always know the present pay rate at any one time, the future of asset prices is always clouded by uncertainty. It is never a good idea to allow tax considerations to dominate investment decisions.

CGT rates are simple, with the exception – for entrepreneurs (see 'Running your own business', page 138) the rate is 18 per cent of your profit.

inflation in the economy, irrespective of the growth or otherwise in the worth of assets such as shares or property.

### The annual allowance

Everyone – and this includes the under 18s (see box, above) – has an annual tax-free allowance to set against gains from selling or giving away investments and possessions. The allowance was the first £10,100 of gains in 2009–10 and the same in 2010–11. Each year, this allowance rises by around the rate of

❝Everyone has an annual tax-free allowance to set against gains from selling or giving away investments and possessions.❞

## Case Study | Joanna and Sheba

Joanna earns £50,000 a year and has £100,000 to invest. She places this in an investment trust, which pays no dividends but which grows by 7 per cent. She sells after one year and, ignoring costs, she has a profit of £7,000. This is within her annual exemption, so she pays no tax.

Sheba also earns £50,000 a year and has £100,000 to invest. She puts this into high yielding bond funds, which pay out £7,000 gross in dividends. She has to add this to her income where it is taxed at her top rate – 32.5 per cent. She has to pay £2,275 in Income Tax compared to nothing for Joanna. Her investment strategy would normally be seen, however, as being less risky than Joanna's.

Trusts also receive an annual tax-free allowance but this is set at half the individual standard rate – in 2010–11, it is £5,050. There is an exception for trusts set up for people with disabilities as these receive the full annual individual allowance.

Providing you use the allowance to the full each year, it is worth around £1,700 in cash saving terms. Of course, it is double that for a married couple or those in a civil partnership as assets can be passed freely between partners in such relationships.

" Providing you use the allowance to the full each year, it is worth around £1,700 in cash saving terms. "

### Calculating the gain on a taxable asset

Working out the gain you make on a taxable asset is comparatively straightforward. You subtract the purchase price (including costs such as commission and any other allowable expenses) from the price you receive on a sale. Whatever that produces can be reduced by capital losses.

To work this out, take your final figure and subtract the annual CGT allowance: £10,100 in 2010–11. You then pay 18 per cent on what is left.

 For more information about Inheritance Tax updates, see the Which? website: www.which.co.uk/advice/inheritance-tax-explained/index.jsp.

## Establishing a purchase price

It is generally easy to find the purchase price of property – sale prices are part of the normal documentation. The worth of quoted shares and similar investments can be checked with the London Stock Exchange Daily Official List (often with some difficulty, however, as many shares may have been divided or consolidated or renamed). Unquoted shares may be more problematic.

HMRC has a Share Valuation Service (see below for the website and telephone helpline details), which will come to an agreement with you. The final figure is usually based on balance sheet assets or what a typical firm in the same business with the same turnover would have been worth.

Establishing the purchase price of other assets, such as works of art, may be even more difficult – there is no accurate way of knowing what the price of something unique you acquired with a legacy many years ago might have been if it had been on sale. This may come down to an agreement between you and the tax inspector to use either something similar or an index, such as those available for impressionist paintings, stamp collections or vintage claret.

---

For example, suppose your gain is £20,100. Subtracting the Personal Allowance leaves £10,000. Your bill would then be £1,800 or 18 per cent.

## HMRC INVESTIGATIONS

HMRC is aware that if you regularly buy and sell items – for example, a series of homes you do up – you might be better off claiming each one as a capital gain rather than as income. It is impossible to say where the line is drawn – it may come down to individual factors, such as your main occupation or how often you do this – but HMRC can challenge whether you are making a capital gain and may say you are trading and should pay Income Tax as a self-employed person (see Chapter 3) instead of paying

**❝ If you regularly buy and sell items, you might be better off claiming each one as a capital gain rather than as income. ❞**

 HMRC's Share Valuation Service is at www.hmrc.gov.uk/shareschemes/shares-valuation.htm, or telephone the helpline on 0115 974 2222.

# Tax tips

- Assets can be passed between spouses or civil partners without any tax liabilities. Where possible, it could save tax if assets are passed by a partner who has already used her or his allowance to the other or if an asset is jointly owned and jointly sold by the partners in the relationship. Equally, ensure the allowance of the taxpayer with the higher personal rate is used up first wherever possible.

- Investments designed for capital growth rather than income, such as certain unit and investment trusts, can help you take advantage of your annual CGT exemption, provided you sell them. But they may prove riskier – shares can go down as well as up and shares without dividends tend to be more volatile. Zero coupon investment trust shares were sold around seven to ten years ago to come up with a low risk way around this – but their construction proved fragile and many investors lost out, finding their investments were only worth a few pennies for each pound they invested.

- Where possible, try to spread out gains over more than one tax year to maximise your annual allowance. Selling some of a shareholding just before the 5 April year-end deadline and then more just after is one way. Some takeovers of public companies offer 'loan notes' instead of an immediate cheque. Loan notes spread the value of the shares you have cashed in for the bid over a number of years – often four or five – so you can make better use of annual allowances. Loan notes pay interest during this period.

- Where a takeover is paid for with new shares in the name of the acquiring company, there is generally no CGT liability. But the new shares are counted as if you acquired them on the same day and at the same price as the old ones they replace.

- You can no longer sell profitable shares or similar assets one day and then repurchase them the next – a process that is known as 'bed and breakfasting' – to establish CGT-free sales by using your annual allowance. You must now leave at least 30 days between the sale and any subsequent purchase of the same investment. This could create a risk – the shares might soar in value over that month and you would lose out.

- But there is nothing to stop you buying other shares – perhaps very similar to the ones you have sold. In the unit and investment trust world, for example, it is very easy to find similar investments from another fund manager to those you have sold – the most obvious example is the index tracking fund. Or you could sell shares in Bank ABC and then immediately purchase shares in Bank XYZ – companies with a similar profile tend to move up and down on the stock market roughly in line.

141

If you dispose of assets that could be liable for CGT that amount to four times or more the annual CGT exemption (£40,400 in 2010-11), you must notify the tax inspector on your self-assessment annual return, whether or not tax is payable. This may also enable you to establish a loss to use against future capital gains.

CGT. The same would apply to persistent online auction traders.

## MAKING A LOSS

Not all investment or business decisions end up profitably. If you lose money, you deduct these sums from your gains. If your losses exceed your taxable gains – the amount over the annual tax-free level – these remaining net losses can be carried forward to be set against profits in subsequent years to reduce these future tax bills to the tax-free level.

There is no time limit to holding these losses, but they have to be claimed no later than five years and ten months after they were incurred. Shares in

companies that go bust are said to be 'of negligible value'.

You cannot go 'backwards', so if you have a loss this year, you are not allowed to deduct it against CGT due from a previous year. The one exception to this rule is when you die, when your executors or personal representatives can look back for up to three years to see if more recent losses can cut the tax bill.

## CAPITAL GAINS AND YOUR HOME

Normally there is no CGT on profits you make on your only or main home. But you might be liable if you develop any part of it so it can be sold separately – effectively if it ceases to be the same property as the one you bought. This would include turning it into bedsits or selling off land over and above the one acre allowed. It would not take in normal improvements, such as loft extensions or building an extra room at the back or side.

**❝ You might become liable for CGT on your home if you develop a part of it to sell separately. ❞**

For more details on when your home may become liable for CGT, see pages 164-5. See also the *Which? Essential Guide: Property Investor's Handbook.*

# The tax bill you leave behind

The two 'inevitables' of Benjamin Franklin's famous quotation, 'In this world, nothing can be said to be certain except death and taxes' come together in Inheritance Tax (IHT). Property and share prices may have taken a tumble, but IHT will still hit the estates of many people. There is also always the chance that values will recover again in the future – IHT planning is a long-term process.

# Working out the IHT bill

We'd all like to be certain our families are as financially secure as possible when we die. For many people, the thought that their children and grandchildren will be provided for – perhaps better than they ever were – with what they leave behind will be a comfort in what can be a difficult and trying time. But IHT now hits a growing number of legacies.

## HOW TO CALCULATE INHERITANCE TAX (IHT)

IHT is in most respects a 'death duty'. And these taxes have been around for almost ever and ever – previous death duty incarnations have included estate duty and capital transfer tax.

It is also, in one way at least, a very simple tax on what you leave behind when you die – this is known as your 'estate'. Working out the mathematics on the amount due on a taxable estate is easy. There is just one 'free slice' – it's £325,000 in the 2010–11 tax year and one flat rate – 40 per cent.

The 'free slice' exempt amount has already been announced for the following year (see right), although these future figures cannot be totally guaranteed as a change of government or a change of policy could alter each and every aspect of the tax. Whatever anyone's view of IHT, all involved agree it is 'politically sensitive'. If you have any doubts, just look at the number of media articles on the subject of its 'fairness'. But fair or not, IHT is what we have.

Once you subtract the exempt amount, virtually everything that's left in the will and available to be passed on to beneficiaries (with the exception of certain donations – see details later in this chapter – and some other exceptions) is taxed at a flat 40 per cent. There are no lower or starter rates.

## LEGAL COUPLES GET TWO ALLOWANCES

If you are married or in a civil partnership (but not any other form of relationship), you now no longer have to set up complicated trusts or otherwise jump through hoops to ensure that both of you will each qualify for a full IHT allowance. Since October 2007, legally joined couples can effectively transfer their allowance to the second one to die.

### How much tax is payable?

| Tax year | IHT-free limit |
|----------|----------------|
| 2009-10 | £325,000 |
| 2010-11 | £325,000 (no change) |

This saves couples from worrying about how the tax might be paid when the first one dies. Often, the great bulk of a couple's wealth is in the value of their home. Finding the money to pay tax might mean selling the family home, scraping the money together from scarce savings resources, being forced to use equity release schemes (where you sell your home for less than its value but can live in it for the rest of your life) to free up capital or borrowing from family.

The alternative to this was to set up a trust in each of the couple's wills. This involved legal costs and necessitated a certain amount of legal sophistication. Many people in this position left wills without such valid trusts. There was also the fear that HMRC would challenge the trust, either because it was badly drafted by a solicitor or as part of a general clampdown on such devices.

## How the new rules work

Under today's rules, the estate of the second to die of either marriage or legal partnership will qualify for two slices of IHT allowances. And the level of the allowance will be calculated according to what it is when the second person dies.

If the first person died in the 2007–8 tax year (when the old rules were still in existence), then the tax-free allowance would be £300,000. If the survivor were to die in the 2010–11 tax year, the allowance for that person would be £325,000 (see How much tax is payable?, opposite) – a total of £625,000.

Now, however, provided the first to die leaves enough to the survivor, the twin

allowances are calculated at twice the level when the second person dies. In the case of the second dying in 2010–11, then it would be twice £325,000 – £650,000, or £25,000 more than under the old system, even if the couple had maximised its use with trusts.

This new system does not apply to couples who divorce, but the double allowance for couples does apply, no matter when the first person died. So the estate of someone who lost his or her spouse in 1980, well before the introduction of IHT in 1984 and 27 years before this rule change, could claim the full amount of IHT allowance for both spouses. This is at whatever the allowance rate is when the second spouse dies.

You cannot claim this double allowance if the first to die used up all his or her tax-free allowance. But if only 50 per cent were used up, then the estate will be able to claim half of whatever the allowance level is when the second person dies.

## ❝The rules do not apply to couples who divorce.❞

## Maximising the benefits

The double allowance works best when everything is left to the survivor. Bequests to other family members will use up all or part of the allowance. Many people will now have to revise their wills to ensure as much as possible is left to the survivor. This can be helpful when there is an informal understanding between the couple (this cannot be in

## How much will it cost?

| Value of estate (2010-11) | Amount of tax to be paid | % of total wealth taken in tax |
|---|---|---|
| Up to £325,000 | 0 | 0 |
| £350,000 | £10,000 | 2.8 |
| £400,000 | £30,000 | 7.5 |
| £450,000 | £50,000 | 11.1 |
| £500,000 | £70,000 | 14 |
| £600,000 | £110,000 | 18.3 |
| £700,000 | £150,000 | 21.4 |
| £800,000 | £190,000 | 23.7 |
| £900,000 | £230,000 | 25.5 |
| £1,000,000 | £270,000 | 27 |

a will or other legal document) that the survivor will give amounts to other family members as a potentially exempt transfer (see pages 153–4). Then, providing the survivor lives for seven years, the entire amount of such bequests fall out of IHT.

## WILL YOU HAVE TO PAY?

Property prices are falling at the moment, but the value of the roof over your head could still push what you leave into the IHT zone – the average price in some areas is still higher than the zero rate allowance. And if you add in savings and the value of other items in your estate, you could still be caught, even if you live in a neighbourhood with lower than average house prices.

In general, the tax-free IHT allowance is up-graded each year roughly in line with inflation. So, even though shares, property and other asset prices are

**❝ The most effective way of cutting an IHT bill is to ensure there is little left in your estate when you die. ❞**

currently depressed, there is always the possibility that they will recover at some time in the future.

## GIVING IT ALL AWAY

The most effective way of cutting an IHT bill is to ensure there is little or nothing left in your estate when you die. In reality, there isn't much you can easily do to reduce the amount of tax your estate will have to pay when you die. The only real ways to reduce your tax bill are to spend your money, or to give it away. The serious problem with 'giving it away' within the rules (and these follow on pages 149–52) is not so much what you will live on but where you will live.

In a nutshell, you can give away as much as you want and, providing you live at least seven more years and the gift fits the HMRC definition of a gift, it will fall out of the IHT calculation.

But the most significant slice of most people's wealth is contained in the value of their home. Selling it is an option as long as you can arrange somewhere else to live, which is attractive. Equally, for many, the savings and investments they own provide a necessary stream of income to boost their pensions. Without this money, they would be hard pressed.

So, it may not be easy to give away things or money unless you already have plenty in reserve on which to live, unless you are prepared to take a big dive in your living standards. However, there are some things that everyone can at least consider, but there are also 'IHT solutions' that can go wrong if you aren't careful.

## WHAT GOES INTO THE IHT BILL?

IHT is first calculated on what you leave behind in your estate – whether or not there is a valid will. This includes the value of various assets.

- Property
- Investments
- Bank accounts
- Savings accounts

- Physical objects, ranging from original works of art to your old car
- Some insurance policies (see box on life insurance policies and writing in trust on page 151)
- Some business assets (see pages 159–60)
- Almost anything else of worth including, in theory at least, the second-hand value of your old clothes.

Significantly, the computation also includes investments that were tax free during your lifetime, such as ISAs or Venture Capital Trusts.

Add back to this the value of certain gifts that you made during the last seven years of your life and any other 'gifts' that HMRC will not view as gifts as they are not considered genuine gifts within current law. All this gives a total sum from which to start the computation.

The tax bill you leave behind

### Tax tip

The estate of anyone who dies on active war service is IHT free. The courts have held that this applies to those who return home and later – possibly many years later – die because the wounds they received on military action hastened their death. The value of medals for valour awarded to the person who died and not sold at the time of death is also IHT free. Additionally, compensation sums paid to survivors of the Holocaust and of Japanese prisoner camps escape the tax.

## WHAT YOU CAN TAKE AWAY

Firstly subtract the IHT-free slice. Then take away anything that you have left to your legal spouse or to your civil partner. No matter how large the sum is, this is always IHT-free, unless the transfer is made to a non-domiciled spouse or partner. However, this does not extend to unmarried partners whether heterosexual or same-sex, no matter how long established the relationship might be.

From this figure, subtract the cost of your funeral and any associated ceremony, the value of any debts to banks, credit card companies, mortgage lenders and similar organisations, and any donations given to good causes – see the Ask the expert box on page 150 for what constitutes a good cause. Certain business assets may also be out of the computation (see pages 159–60). What's left is taxable at 40 per cent.

## Writing a will can cut your bill

Making a valid will can help reduce or wipe out an IHT bill. A will allows you to leave your money to your spouse or civil partner or to charitable causes in the way you want rather than falling foul of the laws of 'intestacy' (these apply where no valid will exists), which insists your estate is divided up in a fixed and rigid fashion. Giving your money in the way you want to a legal partner or a charity can cut the tax take.

But all is not necessarily lost if there is no will. Although it involves extra work and legal expenses, if all the beneficiaries created by the intestacy agree, a will can be created after someone dies. An existing will can also be redrafted in some circumstances, again needing the agreement of all concerned.

It can sometimes be better for all those still living to tear up a will and start again. For instance, many people leave money to their children who may themselves be retired, approaching old age and worrying about their own IHT position. In these circumstances, it might be better if there was 'generation skipping' – leaving the money to grand- or great-grandchildren instead (possibly in some form of trust to prevent youngsters going out and spending it all in one wild shopping spree!).

Changing a will in this way is known as a 'deed of variation' and you have two years from the death of the person concerned in which to effect this. If you decide to go down this route, you will need expert legal help.

 For more information on wills and probate, especially with regard to a deed of variation, see the *Which? Essential Guide* to *Wills and Probate*.

# What you can give away

You can make certain gifts, including some on a regular annual basis, without worrying how long you will live. These values were set in 1984 and have never changed – so they look totally outdated now. Contrast these with the other type known as 'gifts with reservation' – these will only be tax free if you live seven years or longer.

## GIFTS THAT ARE ALWAYS TAX FREE

Some gifts are always free of tax, even if you die within seven years or even seven days or seven minutes of making them. These include marriage gifts (see right) and a number of small gifts up to a fixed value.

You can give an unlimited number of gifts of up to £250 each year to different people free of IHT. However, you can't give someone a tax-free gift in the same year as giving him or her a tax-free wedding gift. Nor can you give the same person more than one gift in the year if the total value tops £250. This gift does not have to be in cash, it's the value that counts.

Every person can give away £3,000 each year free of IHT. If you don't use this allowance one year you can carry it forward to the next tax year, but after that it expires and is of no further use. So if you didn't make the donation in 2009–10 you can give away £6,000 in 2010–11. You are allowed to give someone a wedding gift (see right) and a £3,000 annual gift (or part of it) in the same year.

## WEDDING AND CIVIL PARTNERSHIP GIFTS

How much you can give to a couple getting married depends on your relationship with the people getting married or contracting a civil partnership. These gifts must be made before or at the wedding – they do not count for this exemption if they are made later on.

Trying to get around these limits with multiple gifts – such as several of £250 to one person – or many gifts of £250 to many persons who then each pass the cash on to the same third person is tax evasion and therefore illegal.

- Parents can each give £5,000 tax free to the couple. It does not matter whether the child getting married is legitimate, illegitimate or a stepchild.
- Grandparents can each give £2,500 tax free to the couple.
- Unrelated people can each give £1,000 tax free to the couple.
- You can also give to good causes – see Ask the expert, below.

## " Wedding and civil partnership gifts must be made before or at the wedding. "

## MAKING REGULAR GIFTS OUT OF INCOME

As well as spending as much as you like on yourself – the 'growing old disgracefully' option where you have as much fun as you can handle – you can also make regular payments elsewhere. These might include help for a child or grandchild's education or making financial provision for a less well-off relative or friend.

This money has to come from income rather than savings. The rule is that the amount you give is over and above the income you need to maintain your

## Ask the expert

### What counts as a good cause?

The most obvious good causes are registered UK charities - there are many tens of thousands and you can select whichever you want. You cannot, however, give money directly to foreign registered charities, although some have UK 'subsidiaries' to which you can donate money, either in your lifetime, or in your will without any IHT worries. Beyond this category, there are many other organisations that count as good causes.

- You can give as much as you want to community amateur sports clubs, whether they have charitable status or not - the important factor is that they do not seek to make a profit or that any profit they make is returned to the club to encourage further sporting activities in the community.
- You can donate to certain national institutions, such as the British Museum, the National Gallery, the National Trust, English

Heritage (and the equivalent organisations in Scotland, Wales and Northern Ireland). These donations can be in cash or kind - you could, for instance, give a painting or sculpture that the museum wants.

- You can make gifts of 'heritage property', such as paintings or archives or historic artefacts or buildings, to non-profit making local museums and galleries.
- You can give UK land to registered housing associations.
- You can give money to 'established' political parties - in practice this means the main parties with a presence at Westminster (the European parliament does not count).
- You can leave shares in a company you own or largely own in a trust for the benefit of most or all of the employees who will then control the company.

## Life insurance policies and writing in trust

Check that all life insurance policies that will pay out on your death are 'written in trust'. This will ensure that their value passes straight to your family (or other beneficiaries), avoids your will and therefore is not liable for IHT.

This is a relatively simple procedure, which might have been carried out automatically by the life company when you took out the policy. But if not, it can be easily added in to the legal documentation in your policy.

Premium payments into life insurance policies do not count for IHT. Nor do payments to purchase annuities – plans that turn a lump sum into an income for the rest of your life (and possibly that of a partner).

There are a number of insurance policies designed to protect your estate by paying IHT-bills if you make a gift and fail to live long enough to qualify under the seven-year rule. These will be written in trust. The premiums for these plans count as regular spending out of income and are outside the IHT rules. These require a specialist independent financial adviser.

## Case Study  Angela and Helena

Angela and Helena are civil partners. They have a house worth £500,000 and each has savings of £300,000.

If Angela leaves everything to Helena, there is no IHT payable on her death. Angela wants to leave £50,000 in cash to each of her six grandchildren (which comes to a total of £300,000) and has told her partner of this wish. Helena is not obliged to follow this but intends to do so.

When Angela died in March 2010 (when the IHT allowance was £325,000), Helena inherited everything free of IHT. She then gave the six grandchildren £50,000 each. If she then survives Angela by at least seven years, the £300,000 given to the grandchildren will be outside the IHT net.

When Helena dies, her estate will claim her Personal Allowance (whatever it may be) plus an equivalent sum for Angela.

Assuming the rate is then £400,000, the estate will be able to shelter £800,000 from IHT. Add back the £300,000 to the grandchildren, and the couple have £1.1 million outside of IHT. This is equal to their entire joint wealth in March 2010.

There has been no need to involve lawyers in trusts. But both Angela and Helena must have a valid will leaving everything to the other party otherwise they could fall foul of intestacy (where no will is left) rules, which might distribute the estate in a way different to their wishes. This would have meant paying more in tax.

151

## Living together won't reduce IHT

If you live together, no matter for how long and whether there are children or not, and you aren't married or in a civil partnership, the ability to transfer assets tax free to a partner on death does not apply.

In these circumstances, IHT is payable when one partner dies if he or she leaves more than £325,000, even if the assets are all left to the survivor.

There is a legal challenge to this ruling in the European court. If successful, it will give unmarried couples the same legal rights (including areas other than IHT) as married people and civil partners. However, this may take several years to be decided and there is no guarantee that the law will be changed. Until then, the only way to make sure that no IHT is payable when you give money and property to your partner when you die is to get married.

Moreover, unmarried partners have no automatic right to inherit anything unless it is specifically left in a will.

normal lifestyle. It does not have to remain constant year-on-year – you might have £3,000 in surplus income one year, which you give to help someone's university fees, and £4,000 the next year, which will pay their fees and then leave something over for the student's living expenses.

But it is generally conceded that there is a grey area as to what constitutes normal spending and what should come out of income and what can be paid out of savings. Many people of any age raid their savings for extravagant holidays that they could not afford out of income, for instance. Other regular gifts can include:

- Maintenance gifts to an ex-wife or husband or former civil partner.

- Money given to dependant relatives; for example, for the care of the old or infirm.
- Money given to children up to the age of 18 years.

### TAX-FREE GIFTS TO LEGAL PARTNERS ON DEATH

A husband or wife or civil partner can give assets, including money, property, valuable works of art and stocks and shares, to their partner free of IHT, no matter how much money or property there is when one of them dies or how much time has passed since the gift was made or what conditions were applied to the gift. It does not matter how long the relationship had lasted – as long as it is legal.

There is a simple rule. Whatever you leave to your legal partner, whether different or same sex, is entirely outside the IHT calculation. HMRC will not want to know. This is one of the remaining tax advantages of 'tying the knot'.

**" If you are married, everything you leave to your partner is outside the IHT calculation. "**

# Potentially exempt transfers

Once you have exhausted all the possibilities contained in the previous section on gifts that are always tax free, it does not mean you can stop giving away money, property or other assets to your family or others. But remember that all these gifts come under the potentially exempt transfer (PET) rules.

No matter how old you are now, any money or property you give away (other than to a trust) before your death is called a PET. This means it is could be free of IHT charges if you live long enough. So if you had given £10,000 to each of your four grandchildren on 1 January 2004 and you lived to 1 January 2011, that £40,000 total comes out of the computation.

But IHT may have been payable had you died within the seven years. The transfer is treated as if it was in your will and the recipient is liable for the tax.

There is a 'sliding scale' so that the longer you survive after making the gift (you have to last at least three years for this to have any effect whatsoever), then the smaller the amount of tax the recipient might have to pay (see the table, below).

**❝ If you die within seven years of making a gift, it will be treated as if it was in your will. ❞**

## The tax payable on a PET if you die within seven years

| Number of years between gift and death | IHT payable |
|---|---|
| Less than 3 years | 40% |
| More than 3 but less than 4 | 32% |
| More than 4 but less than 5 | 24% |
| More than 5 but less than 6 | 16% |
| More than 6 but less than 7 | 8% |
| 7 or more years | No tax payable |

## BE AWARE

These IHT reductions are not nearly as attractive for most people's estates as they might initially seem. The value of any PET made less than seven years before your death is taken first from the estate – chargeable PETs use up your free slice, the IHT-free amount (£325,000 in 2010–11), technically known as the 'nil-rate band' (see the case study, below).

As a rule, the wealthier you are, the more use the sliding scale is to you. You can buy life insurance policies that are designed to pick up the bill if you die within seven years. These can be useful if the PET asset you are giving away is not easily turned into cash – a property or work of art, for instance, as opposed to stocks and shares.

**"A life insurance policy will pick up the IHT bill if you die within seven years, which would be especially useful if the PET asset couldn't easily be turned into cash, such as a work of art or a property."**

## Case Study   John and Jane

John is worth £750,000. If he gives away £250,000 as a PET and lives six years, that amount comes first from his free slice, leaving just £75,000 left in the tax-free zone. If the remainder of his estate is worth £500,000, then the tax bill is still calculated on £425,000 (£750,000 less the IHT allowance of £325,000) remains at £170,000, exactly as it would have been if the £250,000 had been left in his will. The taper is worthless here.

Jane also has assets worth £750,000, but she can afford to be even more generous in her lifetime. She gives away £600,000 to her family six years before her death. The first £325,000 comes out of the tax-free slice, leaving £275,000 to benefit from the tax taper. This £275,000 is taxed at 8 per cent (£22,000), while the remaining £150,000 is taxed at the full 40 per cent, giving £60,000. The total bill is £82,000 compared to the £170,000 that John's estate will have to find.

# Unconditional gifts

Whether you give something away under the gift exemption rules, such as a wedding/civil partnership ceremony present, or you make a potentially exempt transfer (PET), the gift must be given without any conditions attached. The donor must abandon any control or interest in the asset.

## MAKING A CLEAN BREAK

A PET is only tax free if there are no strings attached to the gift. It must be a clean break where the donor cannot impose conditions. The most obvious example of this is if you were to give your home to your children but want to continue to live in it. It's not tax free if you continue to live in a property you have given to someone, or if you continue to benefit from an asset – a painting or a piece of furniture. HMRC calls these 'gifts with reservation of benefit' and no matter how long you live, IHT is always payable. Gifts must have a clean break.

If you pass ownership of your home to your children but still continue to live in it, HMRC will count it as though the transfer has never been made, unless it can be shown that you have paid a commercial rent for the privilege of living there. This rent will be taxable in the hands of the recipients.

There is more than just tax to consider. Once you have given away your home to your children, they own it and it becomes one of their assets. If they die, it will be taxable as part of their estate.

### Jargon buster

**Gifts with reservation of benefit**
A gift where the giver retains the right either to use it or ask for it back without payment or at a non-commercial rate

Statistically, however, it is more likely they might become bankrupt or divorce. In either case, this property would become part of their assets for the bankruptcy agreement or any divorce settlement. So, it may have to be sold to meet these obligations, even if you are still living in it. Of course, if you fall out with your children or fail to pay your rent on time, you could be evicted as well.

To make matters worse, if and when your children sell the property after your death and it isn't their main home, they will then have to pay CGT on any increase in value.

Attempts to do this often result in more tax being paid, rather than less.

155

## A few exceptions

You can, however, have some limited enjoyment of assets you have given away. If you give away your home to your offspring, you could stay there for a few nights on visits. And HMRC can be compassionate if you have to move in with your children for care purposes when suffering a terminal illness.

On a lighter note, if you gave a work of art to someone, you could look at it when making normal visits – it does not have to be covered with a cloth.

## PRE-OWNED ASSETS TAX (POAT)

From 6 April 2005, there has been a new weapon in HMRC's armoury against IHT avoidance – the pre-owned assets rule. Here you may have to pay Income Tax at your highest personal rate on the benefit of any property you formerly owned that you continue to benefit from.

These 'pre-owned assets' include money you have lent to someone to buy something you are benefiting from, like a house. You don't have to pay any tax if you are paying the full market rent on the property or are using an **equity release scheme**.

The amount of Income Tax you pay is 5 per cent of the value of the asset or the rental value of the land. If this is less than £5,000, it is tax free.

Instead of paying Income Tax, you can choose for the asset to be included in your estate and pay IHT on it when you die. You need to decide by the end of January in the year following the end of the tax year when tax was due (31 January 2011 for gifts made in the 2008–9 tax year, for example).

## Bending the rules

Over the past few years, there have been a number of schemes marketed by accountants, solicitors and insurance companies – often costing many tens of thousands of pounds – which promise purchasers they can have their cake and eat it. Most of these schemes are complex – each seemingly more convoluted than the previous – as well as being expensive.

Do they work? Some have worked in the past but sometimes only at the cost and time of fighting HMRC through the courts. And even when HMRC loses, it will often try to rewrite tax laws later on to ensure that the loophole is closed forever and no one else will qualify. This usually means that those who have bought into the scheme, but are still alive, will have to abandon their expensive legal agreements as worthless and either reconcile themselves to paying the tax or finding an even more complex way around the rules (together with a whole new set of legal and accountancy fees).

Some items are now caught by the pre-owned assets rule (see above).

In many cases, the IHT option can be better. It's pain later rather than punishment today and don't forget that this can only be levied on death and that no tax is set in stone for all eternity. In some cases, this rule can apply back to 1986, because if you live for a long time, the annual Income Tax bills will mount up – and there is always a chance that IHT will be abolished or radically rewritten.

**❝POAT is payable if you continue to benefit from any property you formerly owned.❞**

## SHOULD YOU PUT YOUR TRUST IN A TRUST?

Trusts are legal devices that separate ownership from control – a basic example is a sum of money given to someone who does not have the mental capacity to control the asset would be put in a trust so the trustees can decide how the money is invested and how it is used.

In some cases, trusts can be used to try to remove money or property from your estate. Putting money into a trust may reduce the amount of IHT that will be payable when you die. However, changes to the IHT rules mean that from March 2006 in most cases if you put more than the IHT-free threshold into a trust, you have to pay 20 per cent tax straight away – HMRC call this a 'chargeable transfer'.

If you die within seven years of putting the money in to trust and it is above the tax-free threshold (£325,000 in 2010–11), your executor then has to pay another 20 per cent.

Trusts are complicated, the rules can change and you will have to calculate any charges when the asset goes into the estate against the potential IHT bill and the legal costs associated with setting up the trust. Trusts are not a do-it-yourself option. You will need to get professional advice. An increasing number of types of trust have been ruled against by HMRC and the courts in recent years.

To find out more about trusts and trustees, see the *Which? Essential Guide* to *Giving and Inheriting*. For some basic help, see also: www.direct.gov.uk/en/ MoneyTaxAndBenefits/Taxes/InheritanceTaxEstatesAndTrusts/index.htm.

## OTHER OPTIONS FOR YOUR HOME

Instead of giving away the property, many will downsize their home and move to somewhere smaller. This would allow you to release equity in the original property and give it to your children. If you live for at least seven years after giving the money, it is free of IHT as it is treated as a PET – see the case study, below. Bear in mind, however, that downsizing may not be worthwhile in some cases. Moving can be expensive with stamp duty land tax to pay (see page 166) as well as estate agency fees and legal costs.

## FREEZING YOUR ESTATE

If you wish to give away assets to your family during your lifetime but fear you might not live the full seven years for it to turn from a PET into the tax-free zone, then consider buying a life policy written in trust for your children or grandchildren.

This effectively freezes the amount of the gift to its value when purchasing the policy, preventing any increase in the tax liability. Using an insurance-based investment also frees the holder from any individual CGT bill (insurers pay this tax directly).

### Case Study  Charlotte

Charlotte owns a house worth £425,000. If she owns it when she dies, her estate would have to pay £40,000 in IHT, assuming she had no other assets whatsoever (and ignoring funeral costs).

This is calculated as follows. The first £325,000 is the tax-free slice leaving £100,000 to be taxed at (40 per cent),

an inheritance of £385,000 for her family. But if Charlotte moved to a smaller house costing £325,000 and gave the released equity of £100,000 to her children or grandchildren, that £100,000 would be taken out of the IHT net leaving no bill to pay - always providing she lives for at least seven years after making the gift.

# Giving away a business

There are special rules for passing on business assets to your heirs. But not everything that you might consider a business counts for this – buy-to-let properties, for instance, are excluded – and some assets, which you may not consider to be a business, are included in this definition.

## UNDER WHAT CIRCUMSTANCES DO YOU NOT PAY TAX?

You can give away a business and not pay any tax (or a reduced amount of tax) as gifts of businesses qualify for business property relief up to 100 per cent. This will enable you to pass on the family firm to the next generation or the one after that without having to worry about IHT costs, which might probably involve breaking up the business to meet the HMRC bill. And a broken-up business may turn out to be worth less or even worthless.

The rule covers shares in unquoted companies – often the way that family businesses are set up – and unincorporated businesses' (an ownership structure such as a partnership or a sole trader). The unincorporated business has to be solely or very significantly owned and controlled by the donor (the owner who gives away the business or shares in the business).

Furthermore, all business assets have to have been owned for at least two years at the time of death – this prevents so-called 'death bed deals' where someone, knowing they have little time to live, buys a business with all their cash. Businesses that count for this IHT special deal include:

- Most normal trading concerns.
- Concerns that are actively involved in managing property, including commercial property and genuine holiday letting enterprises. Holiday lets, including properties that are only rented out for periods of up to one month, must be either actively advertised or hired out through a specialist agency and where you do not stay yourself or let your friends and family stay there for anything less than a commercial rent.

**❝ Gifts of businesses qualify for business property relief of up to 100 per cent, enabling the family firm to be passed to the next generation without paying IHT. ❞**

The business definition excludes buy to let and companies whose sole or main purpose is owning shares in other companies or buy-to-let properties.

If the company in which the donor has a controlling interest is listed on the main stockmarket, the value of this relief is halved – this affects very few people, however.

## Agricultural relief

This tax relief also includes – under a heading known as 'agricultural relief' – the farmland value of owner-occupied farm lands and farm tenancies. This excludes the main residence (the farmhouse), but can include the value of cottages used by farm workers and farm buildings. There are also concessions for landowners who rent out farmland. Woodlands can also count for agricultural relief.

" Tax relief is available on owner-occupied farm lands and tenancies together with land that is rented out for farming. "

# Paying the IHT bill

You have to pay the **IHT** due within six months after the end of the month in which the death occurred. You cannot obtain probate – the ability to distribute the estate in line with the will – until you have settled the tax bill.

HMRC collects IHT from the estate's executors or personal representatives and generally not from the ultimate beneficiaries. The tax payments must be agreed with HMRC before anything can be given to the beneficiaries of the will.

## Who pays it?

If there's a will, it is the responsibility of the nominated personal representative to ensure that the estate is valued accurately and reflects the market value of property and possessions at the time of the death. If more than one person is named as a representative, they are called executors and it is their duty. Where a representative is nominated by a court, because there's no will, for example, they are called a court administrator.

The exception to this rule is where all or substantially all of the estate has been distributed before the death and where the donor did not live long enough for the potentially exempt transfer (PET) to become actually exempt (see pages 153–4). In these cases, HMRC can pursue the recipients.

Where tax is due, executors have to fill in HMRC form IHT200 'Inheritance tax account'. If no tax is due, then this still has to be reported – but use form IHT205 'Return of estate Information' instead. Interest is added to unpaid IHT after the six-month deadline at the standard HMRC rate.

**" Where IHT is payable, it has to be agreed with HMRC and paid before anything can be given to the will's beneficiaries. "**

For more information on dealing with the relevant **IHT** forms and applying for probate, see the *Which? Essential Guide* to *Wills and Probate*.

**161**

## BORROWING TO PAY THE TAX DUE

The executors can use any bank or building society accounts and most National Savings & Investment accounts to pay an IHT bill without obtaining probate. In addition, mainstream shares and similar financial instruments can be sold to meet the cost. But often much of the value of an estate is in a property. For instance, someone with a £500,000 home and nothing else faces a £70,000 charge. And selling a property can be a long, drawn-out affair.

 When someone dies, all their personal tax reliefs die with them. So all the income arising from an estate will then be taxed at the standard rate. Whether IHT is payable or not, this can result in assets being more highly taxed in death than they would be in life. Equally, they may be more highly taxed than in the hands of the eventual beneficiaries – a child with little or no other income, for example. So it is generally worthwhile ensuring the tax is paid as soon as possible to speed up the process of gaining probate and distributing the estate.

In many cases, therefore, executors will need to borrow to pay the tax due. If you borrow to pay the IHT bill, you can offset the interest on the loan for up to a year against the taxable income the estate receives from sources such as bank account interest and share dividends. But this concession is of no help to estates where the sole asset is non-income producing, such as a property that is up for sale.

You can, however, arrange to spread the cost of IHT over up to ten annual equal instalments when it comes to disposing of property, land and certain business assets. Interest will be charged but there are no penalties for repayment ahead of the agreed schedule.

## IF SOMEONE INHERITS ASSETS AND THEN DIES

When somebody inherits something from an estate that has been assessed for IHT and then dies shortly afterwards, there is a special rule known as 'quick succession relief', which can reduce the tax payable on the second death. This helps avoid the same asset being fully taxed twice within a short period of time.

This works on the basis of a sliding scale in the five years after the first death with the first year counting for 100 per cent relief and with each subsequent year losing a fifth of this, falling to a 20 per cent relief in the fifth year.

The value of the asset is, however, adjusted. It may be greater or lesser than its worth in the first will.

# Tax on your property

The home you are buying or have bought outright is probably the biggest single purchase in your life. You may also own a second home as an investment or for holidays or be a buy-to-let landlord. This chapter sets out the essential tax facts anyone involved in property needs to know.

# The home you live in and tax

Except for Council Tax, the home you live in and consider to be your main residence is normally only taxed on two potential occasions – probably when you move in and possibly on your death when it becomes part of the IHT calculation. Otherwise, the main residence is largely outside the tax net. This is most important when it comes to CGT on a profitable sale.

## WHAT COUNTS AS THE MAIN RESIDENCE?

It is essential to know this as the main residence is the only property you can own whose sale will be free of any CGT liability, no matter how much it may have gone up in value or how quickly you sell after buying. All other property, including buy to lets and second homes, is liable for CGT.

In most cases, the main residence will be obvious. It will either be your only home or, if you own a second home, it will be where you normally spend most of your time. Failing that, the main residence is likely to be the property with the higher value and this is generally your main home anyway.

## You do have a choice

But where you have more than one home, you do have a choice. Although it usually is, it does not have to be the property in which you spend the most time or even where you are registered to vote. When you acquire a second property, you can elect which home you want as your main residence by telling the tax inspector. You have two years in which to do this. If you fail to notify the tax authorities within this period, then they will look at the realities, such as where you receive your post or where you live for the majority of the year.

This two-year period starts again every time you change the number of homes you have or their location. And once you have made a decision, it is not written in stone. You can change your mind, backdating the new 'main residence' by up to two years. Your

### Tax tip

You can keep the main residence status indefinitely on your home if you have to move abroad for your employment. And you can retain it for up to four years if you are obliged to move elsewhere in the UK for work purposes. But to qualify, you have to live in the property as a main residence before the posting overseas or elsewhere in the UK and then live in it again before you sell it.

main residence from the tax point of view does not have to be in this country, either. It can be anywhere in the world.

## Two main residences

Under certain circumstances, you might have two main residences. If you move but fail to sell your previous home, you have a three-year window in which to find a buyer for the former home. The same three-year window applies if you divorce and your ex-spouse or civil partner continues to live in the property until it is sold.

You can also designate a home that you are building or totally renovating as your main home. This is useful for self-build enthusiasts who perhaps rent or live in a caravan while they are creating their new residence.

## Selling your garden

Selling off part or all of your garden for housing can be profitable but may not make you popular with your neighbours. You can do this without a CGT liability if it is your main residence provided you are not selling off more than half a hectare (just over one acre). However, if you sell the house first and then part of the land around it to a subsequent purchaser, you face a CGT liability as the home is no longer your main residence.

If you sell the land with the planning permission you have obtained, you still qualify for this CGT freedom. But if you start to develop the land yourself, then you could be liable for a tax bill.

For information on working out your potential CGT liability, see pages 139–42. For more information on co-habiting couples, see the *Which? Essential Guide* to *Divorce and Splitting Up.*

## Stamp duty land tax

| Value of property | % tax |
|---|---|
| up to £125,000 | 0 |
| £125,001 to £250,000 | 1 |
| £250,001 to £500,000 | 3 |
| £500,001 and over | 4 |

\* Properties up to £250,000 are stamp duty free for first time buyers
\*\* Properties over £1m will attract 5 per cent stamp duty from April 2011

## STAMP DUTY LAND TAX (SDLT)

SDLT is levied on the value of the property whenever it changes hands and is charged on the whole value of the property. Unlike Income Tax, it is not 'tiered', so the rate that applies to the purchase price counts for the entire value of the transaction, not just the amount over a threshold.

## Disadvantaged areas

There are some 2,000 postcodes listed on the HMRC website at www.hmrc. gov.uk/so/dar/dar-sd.htm (you can search by postcode or view a list of the wards affected), as 'disadvantaged areas'

## Ask the expert

### How can I reduce stamp duty?

There are substantial savings to be made on property purchases that fall just under one of the thresholds. A property selling at exactly £250,000 brings a £2,500 (or 1 per cent) stamp duty bill. But one selling at £260,000 would cost £7,800 (or 3 per cent) in stamp duty.

The first – and most reliable method – is to try to negotiate the price downwards. Few vendors put a property on the market priced just above a threshold – £249,000 is more attractive than £251,000.

Buyers should also look to see if there is anything that can be sold separately to the house so the property itself falls below the threshold. Pricing separately anything that is portable, such as washing machines, fridges, carpets, moveable furniture, removable solar panels and transportable garden sheds and garden plants, could help reduce the cost of the home. But fixtures such as bathrooms or fitted kitchens or central heating equipment do not count for this as you cannot sell them separately.

Tax inspectors take an interest in home sales that are just under a stamp duty threshold, looking for undeclared cash passing between buyer and seller outside the main transaction or over-valuation of portable items. The worth of many second-hand household items is low.

> " Buyers should look to see if there is anything that can be sold separately to the house so the property falls below a SDLT threshold. "

**Tax tips**

- Students are generally exempt from paying Council Tax, so a property that consists solely of students will normally be council-tax free.
- Other exempt people include those under a mental health act order; someone who is 'severely mentally impaired'; a spouse or civil partner who is a non-British citizen and is therefore not allowed to work or to claim benefits; long-term hospital or care home patients, and members of some religious orders.
- A 'granny flat' where the resident is dependent on the main household is not treated as a separate dwelling.
- Your property may be exempt from Council Tax if it is empty (usually for up to six months), demolished, condemned, or being repaired to make it habitable (up to 12 months). There is no Council Tax to pay if the property has been legally re-possessed by a mortgage lender.

– areas considered to be of social or other deprivation. Here properties valued up to £150,000 are stamp duty free – a potential saving of up to £1,500. But prices in these areas may well adjust to the stamp duty freedom.

## COUNCIL TAX
There are two ways in which a Council Tax bill can be reduced – other than appealing against the valuation of the property itself in the hope it falls into a lower band.

## Second adult rebate
This cuts the bill by 25 per cent. It applies when only one adult lives in the property, or when the other residents are full-time students.

## Council Tax Benefit
This is a means-tested benefit that can reduce a Council Tax bill to zero. Those applying for Pension Credits, Income Support and a number of other means-tested benefits should now be automatically assessed. But you can also apply to your local authority for assessment. Your total savings must be under £16,000 – the value of the house itself, who owns it, or whether there is a mortgage outstanding is immaterial.

# Renting and letting

If you make money letting out spare bedrooms in your own home to lodgers, or you let out your second or holiday home, you will generally have to pay tax on your profits.

This section explains how much tax you might pay as a landlord and the ways that you could potentially reduce the bill. This system is far more akin to running a business as a self-employed person. Buy-to-let properties have a different set of rules that govern the tax you pay and the tax breaks you might claim. Buy to let is considered in the subsequent section (see pages 176–80).

> **" Many people make some extra money letting out a room in their own home to a lodger. "**

 If you have more than one lodger at a time, you could pay CGT on your home when you sell it as it will no longer count as a main residence (even if it is!).

## THE RENT-A-ROOM SCHEME

Many people make some extra money renting out a room in their own homes to a lodger. Providing the room is furnished (it has to be habitable – it is not intended to be luxury but a blanket on the floor will not do) and the annual rental income from a lodger does not top £4,250, this can be tax free if you use the optional Rent-a-Room Scheme. The Rent-a-Room Scheme only applies if you:

- **Let furnished accommodation in your only or main home.** It does not matter whether you own the home outright, are buying it on a mortgage or rent it from someone else – although mortgage payers might need the permission of the home loan company or tenants may have to ask the landlord. You will need to check your insurance policy to see if it allows lodgers – many don't.
- **Live on the premises.** You cannot claim the Rent-a-Room Scheme if you move away, whether for work reasons or other motives.

The £4,250 limit, which has not been upgraded for well over a decade, works out at just under £82 a week. This sum includes any extras you charge for food, washing or cleaning. So, in most cases, it is unlikely to cover more than one lodger.

Where the ownership of the property is shared, and more than one of you owns or rents the house, you can each receive £2,125 per year without paying any tax on it.

Provided that you keep within the Rent-a-Room limits, you do not have to make any declaration to the tax inspector as long as you do not have to fill in a self-assessment form. Otherwise, there is a section on the form to tick if you are claiming under the Rent-a-Room Scheme. You simply select the 'yes' option in the Rent-a-Room section on the land and property supplement to the form.

But Rent-a-Room is not an entirely free gift. Landlords cannot claim any expenses (such as wear and tear, replacement of furniture, lighting and heating) against the rent they charge. In most cases, these expenses would not outweigh the tax freedom. In fact, you would have to make a loss – an unlikely event – before taxpayers are better off outside the scheme. But you can always opt to leave the scheme in a subsequent tax year if you think you would be better off outside it.

While you do need to keep records of the rent you charge, because you cannot claim expenses under the scheme, there is no point in retaining details of what you spend on your lodger or the room.

## What happens if the rent I receive tops the threshold?

Increasingly, rent from lodgers goes above the limit, which was last set in April 1997.

If the rent does go over the threshold, you have two options:

- **You can stay on the Rent-a-Room Scheme** for the first £4,250. Then you pay Income Tax on the balance above that level at your highest personal rate. You cannot offset any expenses against your income.
- **You can opt to leave the Rent-a-Room Scheme** and treat the income from the lodgers in the same way as income from other forms of letting (see overleaf). You will now be able to claim expenses against the rental income you receive.

Which one is better? Unless you can claim expenses – backed up by paperwork such as receipts – in excess of the £4,250 (or £2,125 if shared), then you are better off pursuing the first option.

For more information on the Rent-a-Room Scheme, see the *Which? Essential Guide* to *Renting and Letting*.

**Tax on your property**

169

> **"** You can claim expenses against your rental income, which will help mitigate some tax. **"**

## HOLIDAY LETS

Anyone who makes money from letting property has to pay Income Tax on their profits, but there are different rules depending on whether the property is furnished or not. Your profit is the amount that's left once you've added up your rental income and deducted the running expenses that you have spent on the property – called allowable expenses (see the box on page 172). These

### Case Study  Sophie and Carlotta

Sophie lets a room and supplies meals to a lodger. She charges £120 a week – £6,240 a year and £1,990 above the Rent-a-Room level. She opts for staying on Rent-a-Room for the first £4,250 and paying tax on the balance of £1,990 in the year. If she opted for leaving the scheme, she could claim her £1,500 a year in expenses but she would then have to pay tax on £4,740 – more than twice as much as well as having to deal with the paperwork to establish her expenses claim.

Carlotta is more ambitious and has a larger home. She has three lodgers and provides cordon bleu meals. She earns £30,000 a year from them. Under the Rent-a-Room Scheme, she would have to

pay tax on everything over £4,250, which is £25,750. But she can legitimately show she has expenses amounting to £10,000 a year so, under option two (see page 169), she takes that away leaving tax to be paid on £20,000.

Carlotta's letting venture is such that she is really doing more than just filling up a spare bedroom with a paying guest. She is effectively running an upmarket guest house in her own home. If you do this – whether you choose to call it a hotel, bed and breakfast or guesthouse – and the scope is well beyond the Rent-a-Room, you will be classed as a business and have to declare your income in the self-employment pages of the self-assessment tax return.

 To find out more information on energy-saving equipment in a holiday let, go to www.eca.gov.uk or call the Action Energy Helpline on 0800 585 794.

include the cost of repairs and decoration, but not the purchase price of the property, for example. This section looks at furnished holiday lets. They have a different set of tax rules to unfurnished lettings – furnished lettings are seen as a business while unfurnished lets are an investment in land and property.

## Holiday lettings – the rules

Furnished holiday lettings are treated differently for tax purposes from other property. The house or flat has to qualify – an anti-avoidance measure to prevent people treating their own homes or second homes as businesses (when they could claim a number of expenses against tax) and to stop buy-to-let landlords claiming under this heading. The rules are designed for those who let out country cottages and seaside chalets as a commercial business – not just occasionally for pocket money or lending the property to their friends.

### Minimum letting periods to maximise tax savings

To be eligible as a holiday let, the property has to be in the UK and available for 140 days of the year and let for at least 70 days of those minimum 140 days. Lets of more than 31 days don't count towards these numbers so the tenants must genuinely be short-term holidaymakers. In any case, any longer lets must not exceed 155 days a year.

Rental levels have to be broadly comparable to those in the market – you could not, for instance, let your friends or family stay in the property for £1 a week and still hope to qualify under the 70-day rule.

If the property does not qualify as a holiday let, there are no tax breaks under these rules. There is a chicken and egg dilemma here. If the property does not attract customers, for whatever reason, then it fails the holiday let test, so you cannot claim for items that you may have bought to attract customers in the first place.

## Claiming capital allowances

The main advantage of holiday letting is that you can claim capital allowances against the cost of furnishing and equipping the property. Items could also

Tax on your property

---

### Green tax tip

If you install energy-saving equipment, such as heating and refrigeration, in your holiday let, you could qualify for a 100 per cent first year capital allowance (for contact details, see box on page 173).

---

For more information on capital allowances and what they can mean to your tax bill, see page 68.

## Allowable expenses for holiday lets

Some of the most common expenses you can deduct are:

- Water rates, ground rents and Council Tax.
- Gas and electricity (unless paid by the tenant via a slot meter or similar system).
- Building and contents insurance - you will need to specify the holiday let nature of the property, so premiums will generally be higher.
- The interest you pay on a mortgage to buy the property - but not the capital repayments.
- The amount you pay for services that you buy in, including the

wages of gardeners and cleaners - but you cannot charge your own time if you do some or all of this work yourself.
- Repairs and decoration - but don't forget that you won't get away with gold leaf wallpaper in a low rent small flat.
- Letting and estate agency fees and the cost of advertising for tenants.
- Legal and professional fees in connection with the letting activity.
- Wear and tear of furniture and equipment in a furnished property.

include anything to help maintain the property on a regular basis, such as a lawnmower, vacuum cleaner and a set of ladders. These allowances mean you can charge the value of durable items over their life against tax.

Most holiday lets are from smaller concerns, which can claim 50 per cent of the item's value in the first year and subsequently a quarter of the balance in each succeeding year.

Capital allowances are on top of other running expenses you can claim against the rental income, but you cannot claim both a capital allowance and an expense allowance on the same item at the same time.

Unlike losses from other properties, such as buy to lets, losses from a holiday

let are treated in largely the same way as any other income from self-employment. Losses can be used to reduce tax on any income (not just income from property) in that tax year or previous years. It can also be carried forward, but then it can only be used to reduce income from property and not other income.

## Pay less by deducting expenses

You can reduce the amount of tax you pay by claiming some expenses (but obviously not if you claim under the tax free Rent-a-Room Scheme).

You are allowed to reduce your taxable income by expenses that are incurred 'wholly and exclusively' as a result of letting out property. This is the same test as for running other sorts of business as a self-employed person or in a partnership.

Effectively, you can claim for anything you spend to make the property attractive – for example, the costs of repairs and decoration – and what you spend to ensure you have a tenant, such as letting agent fees and advertising the holiday home. There is a comprehensive list opposite. This means that if you spend £500 on painting and decorating and agent fees of £1,000 in a year, your taxable income would be reduced by £1,500 (£500 plus £1,000).

Many holiday lets are used by owners, their families and friends for part of the year – this is permissible within the minimum availability and minimum letting rules (see page 171). Assuming those periods are not charged at a commercial rent, then you should reduce your expenses claim proportionately.

> **❝ If you are going to be paying tax on the income received from your let, it makes sense to reduce the bill by deducting valid expenses. ❞**

## Case Study  Helena and Martha

Helena and Martha own a seaside cottage that is available through a letting agency for ten months each year. It is generally let during these periods – the odd empty week is used for repairs, maintenance and decoration. So it qualifies as a holiday let.

But two months in the year are blocked out because the couple want to use it privately for themselves and their friends. So they claim 100 per cent of their fees from the letting agency, any legal fees in connection with the lettings, any extra insurance costs because it is let out, and anything else that is totally tenant oriented.

However, the result of much other spending, such as Council Tax, heating, decoration and the mortgage interest, is partly enjoyed by them for two months a year. So they deduct five-sixths of these costs for the ten months of tenant occupation against their rental income, leaving them to pay the one-sixth proportion in line with when they are occupying the property.

 An explanation for 'wholly and exclusively' in relation to self-employed people or those in a partnership is given on pages 66-7.

173

## Other possible deductions

You cannot deduct the cost of the purchase of the property or the cost of making substantial improvements, such as an extension to the property or the cost of making an uninhabitable property habitable. This is known as 'capital spending'.

You can, however, claim for necessary work, such as replacing an old broken bath with a new one – although you should not attempt to upgrade. That said, sometimes this cannot be avoided. For example, you can no longer replace certain types of central heating boiler on environmental grounds or some types of television set as they are no longer made. Their replacements are better, but you have no choice. HMRC should be pragmatic on occasions such as these.

## What if I make a loss?

Losses on holiday letting activities are generally just the same as a loss on any other self-employment business venture. Losses are common when you start up as your costs, such as making a property habitable and mortgage interest, may well exceed your earnings. When this happens, you can offset your loss against other income that year or carry it forward against future income.

If the loss is during the first four years of trading, you can claim against your own income over the three preceding years – with the claim against the earliest year first. This can be useful – perhaps you are downshifting your work – if you were previously paying tax at the top rate and the losses can reduce your tax rate to the basic rate.

## Rental income from overseas

Many people now own villas and flats abroad, which they rent out for periods of the year as a commercial venture. If you do this, you must tell HMRC about rental income you get from holiday properties you own overseas on the foreign supplementary pages of the tax return. You can subtract costs, such as management, legal fees, services and

**❝Losses are common when you start up a holiday let as your costs may well exceed your earnings.❞**

174

Everything in the holiday let tax legislation assumes you are letting out the property or properties on a commercial basis for at least the minimum time period each year.

mortgage interest, from the rental income. You have to use the exchange rate from the time when the rent was received. You cannot use the Rent-a-Room Scheme.

You get a credit (generally an amount you can set against your UK tax) for any tax you have already paid overseas to non-UK tax authorities. The big difference, however, is that you cannot offset any losses you make against your UK income (in the way you can with a UK holiday let). If you make a loss, you can only offset it against rental income from the same property in a future year – this can be rolled forward for as many years as is necessary. You cannot offset it against other property rental income either abroad or in the UK.

If you own several properties in one country, it might sometimes be beneficial setting up a company in that country. But this will depend on the country in question so you should always take independent advice.

Your overseas property will be liable for CGT if you sell it at a profit – unless this is your main residence. It will also count towards the value of your estate for IHT when you die (see Chapter 8).

## Letting out your home while you live overseas

If you let your home while you live abroad, your tenant must deduct basic-rate Income Tax and pay it to HMRC. You then offset the tax you've paid against your tax bill when you complete your tax return. This will reduce the amount you have to pay via your self-assessment. You can also apply for permission to receive your rental income with no tax deducted (as long as you live abroad for more than six months) using form NRL1 'Non-resident landlords – individuals'. This is advisable if you will be living abroad long enough to escape the UK tax net altogether.

## Paying tax

As the holiday let is considered to be a commercial business, you pay tax in exactly the same way as you would for any other self-employment business through self-assessment form SA103. You must also keep records of all your business dealings. But with a holiday let, you must also keep records of when the property was commercially available and when it was let out.

Chapter 10 (see pages 182–207) provides further information on filling in a self-assessment form, tax year endings and keeping records.

## BUY TO LETS AND TAX

Buy to let where you purchase a property to rent it out to tenants on a long-term basis – usually unfurnished – continues to grow in popularity with buy to letters considering it as an alternative investment asset to stocks and shares. Yet the phrase 'buy to let' does not appear in tax legislation.

Buy to let occupies a grey area in the tax world somewhere between running a business (such as owning a shop or renting out holiday flats) and owning an investment (such as stocks and shares). It's not strictly considered a business because you cannot offset losses on buy to let against your other income – as you can do with a holiday let, for instance. But unlike other investments, there are a number of expenses you can set against the income you get from the tenants.

## Taxes to concern you

You have to worry about two taxes:

- **Income Tax** you will have to pay on the income from your tenants, less a number of allowance expenses.
- **CGT,** which is only payable when you sell the property at a profit after taking purchase costs into consideration.

## Income Tax for buy-to-let landlords

The rent tenants pay you is taxed each year. The amount is usually based on the income that is due to you during the tax year rather than on the rent that tenants actually hand over during that year. This means that if a tenant pays you three months' rent in advance on 6 March, only one-third of that falls within the

---

### Tax tip

Buy-to-let landlords can offset the interest costs of their loans against their income from the tenants. You can also use this when you re-mortgage. The re-mortgage can be greater than the original loan providing it is not more than the original value of the property when it became a buy to let. The money from the new loan can be used for any purpose – not just for the property in question. A variation on this is when you move to a new house as your main residence and decide to rent out the old one. Using this rule, you could raise a mortgage on the property's value when it became a buy to let, repay your original residential mortgage and enjoy the balance as a loan where the interest can be deducted for tax purposes.

---

More information on the relevant self-assessment forms, including form SA103, is given on page 183. See also the Which? online help and video for filling in your form: www.which.co.uk/advice/how-to-fill-in-your-tax-return/online-tax-returns-video-guide/index.jsp.

current tax year, so only one third is taxable that year – with the rest falling into the next tax year. This can be particularly tricky if the tenant is late with the rent – you have to account for it because it is due, even though it is unpaid, and pay tax on that, later claiming a refund if the tenant's lateness turns into a bad debt.

The same proportionality applies with expenses. If you pay your annual insurance bill on 6 March, you can only count one-twelfth of that against that year's tax.

This method is called the 'earnings basis' and can involve substantial amounts of mathematics. But provided you keep good records detailing everything on a monthly basis and you can apportion everything across 12 months, it shouldn't be necessary to use an accountant for this.

You will need to send in a self-assessment tax form each year that you own a buy to let, even when there is no tax due.

## What expenses are allowable?

Buy-to-let landlords incur many expenses. Some are allowable and you can offset them against your rental income while others are not – these are 'disallowable' expenses.

*Allowable expenses*
- **Publicity and advertising** of the property – local newspapers, websites and shop windows, for example.
- **Repairs to the property** and general maintenance costs (but see overleaf).
- **Cost of services** provided to your tenants, such as gas and electricity together with any Council Tax that the tenant does not pay.
- **Managing agents' fees,** insurance against tenant delinquency (incidents such as tenants vandalising the property, stealing items, or not paying the rent).
- **Insuring the building and contents.**
- **Interest paid** on any loan taken out to buy the property.

*Disallowable expenses*
- **The cost of buying the property itself.**
- **The capital repayment part** of any mortgage you took out.
- **Expenses involved with buying and selling,** such as legal fees and survey costs.
- **Renovation work,** such as making a property habitable (but see Green tax tips, page 179).

**❝Buy-to-let landlords incur many expenses. Some are allowable, while others are not. ❞**

- **Improvements you have made to the property,** such as replacing an item with one of a higher specification (unless the original specification is no longer available, see Ask the expert, opposite), putting in central heating, or making repairs that you knew about at the time of purchase and which accounted for the property initially coming onto the market at a lower price than it would otherwise have fetched.
- **Any expenses** you run up, such as insurance, Council Tax, heating and security, when the property is not available for letting.
- **The costs of disposing of the property** when you sell (but see Capital Gains Tax, page 180).

## What to do with deposits

Deposits legally belong to the tenant so they are not taxable unless the landlord keeps all or part of the deposit to pay for missed rent or damage. It then becomes the same as any other income and will be taxable.

**" Deposits belong to the tenant so are not taxable unless the landlord keeps all or part of the deposit to pay for the missed rent or damage. "**

## Ask the expert

### How do I account for a furnished property I'm letting?

If you rent out a fully furnished property, you can choose how you claim for the expense of furnishing it. You can claim the replacement cost of furnishings, like cookers and carpets, when they are replaced, but you have to deduct any money you get when you dispose of them. You can't claim money if you make improvements, for example, replacing a washing machine with a more expensive washer-dryer.

The alternative is to reduce your rental income by 10 per cent each year instead of claiming for worn-out furniture and appliances. This would be after you have cut back your rental income to account for bills you pay instead of the tenant, for example, Council Tax or water rates.

Whichever way you do it, once you've decided, you have to carry on that basis as long as you rent out that property.

 For more information on CGT, see pages 134–42, which describes captial gains and how to work out the tax on any investments or assets that you might sell.

## Green tax tips

- Landlords can claim for the cost of loft and certain other insulation fitted before April 2009 up to £1,500 per residential property each year. This is called landlord's energy saving allowance. This cannot be claimed if using Rent-a-Room or furnished holiday lettings. Landlords can also claim for the cost of installing draught protection and putting in a hot water system (where none existed previously). This is not paid in cash but reduces taxable income.

- There are tax incentives to help landlords who convert unused or storage space over shops into habitable accommodation. These are known as 'flat conversion allowances'. The building must not be more than four storeys high and the flat must have its own front door (and not be accessible via the shop).

The property has to have been out of residential use for at least one full year. The flat itself must be built before 1980 and have no more than four rooms (not counting hallway, kitchen, toilet and bathroom).

You can then set all your renovation costs against rent – which you could not do with other premises. If these exceed the first year's rent, then you can carry the costs forward. The rules can be complex and to qualify, the flats themselves must not be 'high value'.

The HMRC website lists maximum weekly rents you can charge – currently £350 a week in Greater London and £150 a week elsewhere – for a one- or two-bedroom flat, and more for larger units.

**❝ There are tax incentives to help landlords who convert unused or storage space over shops into habitable accommodation. ❞**

## Capital Gains Tax (CGT)

You are taxable on the proceeds from the sale less the original price paid for the property. Costs can include fees associated with the original purchase, such as legal and survey fees, which you add to your original price.

You can also add the cost of any improvements that were disallowed under Income Tax rules. You could, for instance, claim the building cost of an extension or a major kitchen refit because both will be reflected in the price you receive for the property.

**❝To claim any flat conversion allowances, the property has to have been out of residential use for at least a year.❞**

## Tax tip

You may be able to avoid CGT if you move into the property before you sell it and declare it as your main residence. But the tax inspector could check to see if this move is genuine.

 For more information on flat conversion allowances, see HMRC link CA43000 'Flat conversion allowance', which leads to separate leaflets covering different subjects.

# Dealing with your tax affairs

This chapter gives you the essential facts you need to know before tackling your tax return. It lays out the advantages and drawbacks of using an accountant or other tax professional. It also tells you what your rights and responsibilities are when dealing with the tax authorities – and how to complain if you believe you have been treated badly.

# Your tax return

Each year, around one-in-ten taxpayers who have to fill in a self-assessment tax form are fined £100 for late filing. Many of those also have to pay further penalties and interest payments, most of which are unnecessary.

## WHO HAS TO FILL IN A TAX RETURN?

You will need to fill out a self-assessment tax return if you:

- Are self-employed, a company director, a business partner, a trustee or a personal representative of someone who has died.
- Receive rental income above £2,500 a year and are not on PAYE, or have taxable foreign income.
- Receive other untaxed income and the tax due on it cannot be collected through PAYE (see page 112).

If you're an employee or over 65, you will have to fill out a return if:

- Your annual income is more than £100,000 or you receive untaxed income of at least £2,500 a year.
- You have annual investment income of at least £10,000 or you claim £2,500-plus a year in expenses.
- You're entitled to some age-related personal or Married Couple's Allowance, but not the full amount (unless your affairs are very straightforward).

If your circumstances change and you receive new income during the tax year (if you start letting a property or take on a paid spare time job, for instance), you must let your tax office know by 5 October following the end of the tax year, so it can decide whether you need to complete a return.

## WHICH RETURN SHOULD I RECEIVE?

Most people on self-assessment receive the main tax return (form SA100), which asks for information on their income from savings, investments, state benefits

 Besides telling the tax inspector of any substantial new source of income that would qualify you for a self-assessment form, you must also report any increase in your earnings that could put your savings and investments in line for the top tax rate or if you have any taxable capital gains.

## Fewer taxpayers to receive self-assessment forms

HMRC has realised that the cost of a self-assessment form for many people with simple affairs is excessive compared to the tax raised. Such people might include higher-rate taxpayers on PAYE (earning up to £100,000) with just a work perk (such as a car or private medical insurance), or interest from one or two savings accounts.

HMRC has identified 1.6 million people in this category. If you are one, you may receive an 'exit letter' during the tax year, which starts: 'We have looked at your last tax return and do not propose to send you returns in the future.'

This letter is only sent to those people whose forms and payments arrive on time. You can continue to fill in the self-assessment forms should you wish.

You must let HMRC know as soon as there are any significant changes in your circumstances since you last filed a self-assessment form. The exit letter gives a list, but changes centre on earning more than £2,500 from a variety of sources.

Remember that it is your responsibility to report changes and to claim refunds should your circumstances change.

You may find that you are sent form P810 every third year. This is a reminder that you must report certain changes in earnings outside of PAYE, such as untaxed interest or property income.

Form P810 enables HMRC to check your income to ensure you pay correctly. You may be sent this form, for instance, if you make a Gift Aid payment of more than £300, or where there is a change in the tax relief you claim on pensions.

and pensions. The forms that are sent out from 6 April 2009 cover the 2008–9 tax year.

It also covers allowances and tax reliefs you might be eligible for during the tax year, such as expenses from work. But unless all your income comes from savings and/or pensions you will also have to complete one or more of the nine supplementary forms. These are:

- SA101 Employment
- SA102 Share Schemes
- SA103 Self-employment
- SA104 Partnerships
- SA105 Land and Property
- SA106 Foreign Income
- SA107 Trusts
- SA108 Capital Gains
- SA109 Non-Residents
- SA110 Tax calculation summary.

In addition, there are special versions of some of the above forms for special cases, such as ministers of religion, Lloyd's of London underwriters, members of parliament and also special forms for Scottish MPs, members of the Welsh Assembly and the Northern Ireland legislative assembly.

## FILING THE FORM

You have a choice of ways of completing and returning the self-assessment form – from hi-tech to delivery by hand.

## Online filing

Internet filing has improved substantially since the early days when downloading the software took nearly all day. Filing online enables you to fill in the numbers and let the computer add them up for you, telling you what you owe (or when and how much you are due as a rebate).

You can file online up to the deadline of 31 January, but bear in mind that you also have to pay any tax due by 31 January or you will be charged interest.

You must, however, register for online filing at least a working week ahead of the date on which you intend filling in the form. This gives HMRC sufficient time to be sure it can issue you with a password to your home by post.

If you don't want to rely on the HMRC website, there are a number of software packages you can buy that will do the work for you. You can then print out the results and send them off by post or hand deliver to your local tax office before 31 October. But if you want to file online using the software, you will still have to register. Some outside software, such as TaxCalc, can be more user friendly than the HMRC website and cover a greater variety of special filing needs.

## Paper returns

If you don't have access to the internet or prefer to fill out a paper return, then, provided you file your return by 31 October, HMRC will calculate your tax bill for you. If you file later than this, you can still ask for your bill to be calculated, but HMRC won't guarantee to let you know how much tax you owe in time for the final deadline of 31 January.

Many tax offices have late-night and weekend openings towards the end of January to receive payment. And you don't have to send it to your tax office – you can hand deliver it at a local office that is more convenient. When 31 January falls on a Sunday, HMRC will announce any special arrangements.

**❝ If you're happy to calculate your own tax, you have until 31 January following the end of the tax year to do so. ❞**

For help with filling in self-assessment forms, call the HMRC helpline: 0845 9000 444 (8am-8pm seven days a week, including bank holidays). For extra forms or help sheets, call the HMRC orderline: 0845 9000 404.

## FILLING IN THE FORM

With the paper self-assessment tax form deadline now falling on 31 October, a record number of people have signed up for online filing – 65 per cent of the tax-paying population. Here we list – and answer – some of the most common questions taxpayers ask.

## How do I register for HMRC's online tax return service?

Make sure you have your Unique Taxpayer Reference (UTR) number (printed at the top of your tax return) and either your postcode or National Insurance number.

- Go to the HMRC website for the online tax return service – https://online.hmrc.gov.uk/login – and select 'Register' in the 'New user' section.
- Select 'Self-assessment online' and follow the on-screen instructions.
- Once you have completed the registration process, your unique User ID and Activation PIN will be sent to you by post from the Government Gateway. Allow up to seven working days for them to arrive.

Once you have your User ID and Activation PIN, return to the online address above or go to the main HMRC

**"The HMRC website is designed to give you support for filling in your self-assessment form."**

website at www.hmrc.gov.uk and select 'Self assessment' from the 'Do it online' section and log in using your User ID and chosen password.

From here, follow the instructions to activate self-assessment online. You must do this within 28 days. After this time your Activation PIN will no longer be valid and you will have to start again. Once you have activated the service, you can destroy the PIN.

## What happens if I lose my identity PIN?

HMRC sends out replacement PINs for taxpayers by first class post.

- Go to www.hmrc.gov.uk/sa/using-online.htm and tab up to 'If you have lost your User ID or password'.

## Why rely on the post for sending codes and logins?

Replacement PINs (as well as the original) are posted as this is the most secure method of ensuring that the relevant information is delivered to the correct person.

For more information about registering for the online tax return service, go to www.hmrc.gov.uk/sa/understand-online.htm. See also the Which? online help and video for filling in your form: www.which.co.uk/advice/how-to-fill-in-your-tax-return/online-tax-returns-video-guide/index.jsp.

## What happens if my online PIN does not arrive in time?

Whether it is the first PIN or a replacement, you should allow seven working days for the post to deliver it. HMRC often improved on that in 2008-9, but that time limit remains the rule. However, HMRC did allow taxpayers whose PIN was delayed to file after the 31 January deadline – effectively into the first week of February.

Although the taxpayer would get a £100 penalty notice, HMRC was prepared to treat a late return appeal on 'reasonable excuse grounds' sympathetically where a taxpayer registered before 31 January and filed the return as soon as possible after receiving the PIN (see also pages 189–90).

## What happens if my computer breaks down at the last moment?

Provided you know your PIN, you can file from another computer although with some email systems you need your own machine to receive the confirmatory email from HMRC.

However, if a taxpayer owes no tax on 31 January, the penalty will be nil – any penalty imposed will be removed. So taxpayers faced with a computer crash can avoid problems by paying – or overpaying to be on the safe side – the amount due. The payment date is always more vital than the filing date.

## If I am not sure of a question, what do I do?

- Just click on the green question mark next to the appropriate field. This may answer your query immediately.
- You can also download a copy of the step-by-step guide to filing your online return at the website given below.

## I don't understand the question or the online answer. What should I do?

If you don't understand the question or the answer, then it is unlikely that you will be able to cope with HMRC's difficult to navigate online search facility.

- Try phoning the HMRC helpline on 0845 60 55 999. If you have a landline or mobile call bundle, you can alternatively dial 0161 9319070.

**❝Should your computer break down, you can pay your tax from someone else's PC or Mac. ❞**

HMRC provides a step-by-step guide to filing an online return at www.hmrc.gov.uk/sa/help-using-online.htm. You can also look at the online tax return for self-assessment demonstrator at www.hmrc.gov.uk/demo/index.html.

## I can't see the pages I need to complete my online tax return for self assessment. What is wrong?

HMRC's free online service does not cover all tax circumstances.

- Detailed information on what HMRC's free service covers can be found at www.hmrc.gov. uk/sa/software.htm.

You will find the following pages are not available: minister of religion (SA102M); Lloyd's underwriters (SA103L); trusts (SA107); non-residence (SA109); partnership return and supplementary pages (SA800); trust and estate return and supplementary pages (SA900).

If one of these circumstances relates to you, you may still file your return online, but you will need to use commercial software, such as TaxCalc.

## I am not being offered the pages that I need. Why?

Software (whether commercial or from HMRC) often depends on how you answer earlier questions to decide which pages to present to you later on.

So if you answer questions under the personal details section, which helps tailor the return, incorrectly or miss any out, this then results in a series of questions,

for example on self-employment or buy-to-let income, not being presented.

- Go back to the start, check the answers and correct any mistakes, so the return is then updated.
- More information on tailoring the return can also be found in HMRC's step-by-step guide and software demonstrator (see box at foot of page opposite).

**"The HMRC helpline is designed to sort out your concerns, so if in doubt, use it."**

## I can't move to the next screen because it keeps telling me I've made an error. Help!

The most common reason for error messages is that you have not completed a box, leaving it blank, rather than inserting a '0'.

- Check the questions on that page again and where your answer is nil (so you have ignored the box and left it blank), insert '0' instead.

 **Software suppliers, such as TaxCalc, can be found at www.hmrc.gov.uk/efiling/ sa_efiling/soft_dev.htm.**

## My paper form arrived after 31 October so I have been sent a penalty notice. Will it help if I file online before 31 January?

No. HMRC does not allow two bites at the cherry in this way. But provided you have calculated what you owe correctly, and send in the money before the 31 January deadline, HMRC will have to rescind any penalty provided you appeal.

## Do you have any other tips to help me complete my online return?

- Remember that you need to file your return by midnight on 31 January.
- Set aside adequate time to complete the form, if possible, in a place where you can concentrate on it and not be constantly disturbed. But remember that you can save your form and return to it at a convenient time if you want to take a break.

- Collect together all you need to do your return beforehand. That is your P60, if you are employed or receive a pension, and details of any fringe benefits and expenses. If you are self-employed or have letting income, you will need copies of your accounts and expenses. You will also need your bank statements if you pay interest on your bank account and details of any income from investments and savings.
- When filling in your tax return, round to the nearest pound in your favour – that's income down and outgoings up. Where you are asked to add together income and credits from various sources, ensure you round down the total figure.

**❝ Make sure you have all your paperwork to hand and plenty of time. ❞**

 The online help desk is on 0845 60 55 999 or 0161 931 9070 and the self-assessment helpline is on 0845 9000 444 or 0161 931 9070. These numbers are available seven days a week, 8am to 8pm.

# Tax deadlines

You will be fined if you miss deadlines – and the penalties can mount up. In this section we look at deadlines for delivery of the self-assessment forms, payment on account and making adjustments.

## IF YOU ARE LATE

At the most basic level, HMRC will charge those filing forms after the 31 January deadline an automatic £100 penalty if you have outstanding tax to pay in excess of that amount at the 31 January filing deadline. If your return is still outstanding six months later, you'll be charged another £100. These sums have been unchanged since self-assessment was first introduced more than a decade ago. They are identically applied to both major and minor offenders.

If your return is seriously late, you might also be charged a further penalty of £60 a day, but only where HMRC has permission from the Special Commissioners. If this happens, the penalty can exceed the tax due. This is mainly aimed at tax delinquents rather than those who inadvertently are late with their filing or whose tax bill is low anyway.

You will be charged interest at 7.5 per cent from the date the payment was due as well as a late payment penalty. If you still haven't paid by the following 28 February (one month later), you will be charged a 5 per cent surcharge on the tax due, which goes up by a further 5 per cent of the amount due if you still haven't paid by the following 31 July.

## Tax tip

These penalties can never exceed the tax due. So if you are unsure of the exact amount, or even when you simply have not got all the information together, as long as you overpay, you cannot be fined. For instance, if you have not got the details of a savings account but you think the tax due is around £20, overpay to, say, £50 to avoid a fine. You will eventually get a refund, but you will avoid a penalty for underpayment. All penalties are currently under review.

## Making excuses

Postal strikes, floods, fires and serious illness are among the excuses that may work – they need to be backed up with evidence, such as a medical certificate. But don't bother trying 'my accountant let me down' or 'I can't find the paperwork' or 'I don't have the cash at the moment.'

## COMING OFF SELF-ASSESSMENT

Every year, a number of people come off self-assessment – usually because their earnings have fallen and they have

## Tax calendar

These are the important dates for the 2009-10 tax year.

| Date | What you should do |
|---|---|
| 31 October 2010 | The deadline to file your paper return if you want HMRC to calculate your tax for you. You can still ask it to calculate your tax after this date, but it won't guarantee to have worked out your tax by the final deadline for paying tax, which is 31 January 2011, and so you run the risk of incurring interest and penalties. People who file paper returns and want any unpaid tax under £2,000 to be collected by PAYE must also meet this deadline. |
| 30 December 2010 | Online filers who have PAYE earnings can have overdue tax under £2,000 collected by PAYE provided they meet this date. |
| 31 January 2011 | The final deadline for online tax returns and to pay any tax and National Insurance due. |

dropped out of the top-rate tax band or they have stopped being self-employed. HMRC tries to sift out those in this position. HMRC writes to them to inform them that they should no longer have to fill in an annual return. However, if you feel your circumstances have changed sufficiently, you can write to your tax inspector requesting you be taken out of the self-assessment net.

## HELP YOURSELF

Form filling can be arduous at the best of times. Follow these tips to help yourself:

- **If you are returning a paper form, don't forget to sign your tax return** – it is one of the most common reasons why people get fined. If you send your return in just before the deadline, unsigned, it will be treated as being late.
- **Even if HMRC do the sums for you,** check your tax bill carefully. HMRC can get your details wrong, which might result in you paying too much tax.
- **Avoid paying penalties and interest.** Make sure you get your return back and your tax paid by the final deadline of 31 January 2011 (for the 2009–10 tax year).

**&& Don't forget to sign your tax return – it's one of the most common reasons for a fine. ,,**

- **If numbers aren't your thing,** file your return online as your tax bill will be worked out for you (see pages 177–80).
- **If you want tax you owe to be collected through PAYE,** get your paper return back by 31 October or your online return by 30 December.
- **You can get your return filled in by a tax professional,** but be prepared to fork out about £100 for the privilege.

## PAYMENTS ON ACCOUNT

If you receive income that hasn't been taxed, you have until the 31 January following the end of the tax year to pay up.

So, you may think this gives you time to keep your hard-earned cash out of HMRC's coffers? Think again, the tax rules mean that some groups are asked to make interim tax payments. These are known as payments on account.

Payments on account only apply if you're filling in a tax return. The exemptions (see tax tips, above) mean that if you're employed and receive your other income through bank and building society accounts, you won't have to worry. If you are self-employed or have significant investment or freelance income, you need to understand the system so that you pay the right amount of tax.

### When do you pay?

You have to pay in two equal instalments. The first payment is due on 31 January in the tax year and the second on the 31 July after it in the same year. Any

---

### Tax tips

- You do not have to make payments on account if more than 80 per cent of your previous year's tax bill was met by deductions at source or if the amount owed is £500 or less. This doesn't mean you escape paying the tax – it just simplifies matters. If either exemption applies, you can make a single payment by the 31 January following the end of the tax year (31 January 2011 for the 2009-10 tax year).
- You're responsible for making payments on account by the deadlines, even if you're not prompted by HMRC.

---

balance has to be paid by the following 31 January.

That means for the 2009–10 tax year your first payment is due on 31 January 2011, the second payment on 31 July 2011 and any balance is due by 31 January 2012.

You are responsible for paying by the deadlines. The only exception is where you've submitted your return by 30 September and asked HMRC to calculate your tax, but they haven't sent a statement of account. In this case, the payment is due 30 days from the notification date. But if the payments you're due to make are greater than your tax bill, you can get a rebate at any time. Contact HMRC immediately.

**191**

## What you pay

Normally, each of the two payments (end of January and end of July) is half your previous year's tax bill. This includes Class 4 National Insurance contributions, but excludes:

- Capital Gains Tax
- Student loan repayments
- Any other tax that's been deducted at source (such as through PAYE).

## Working out what you pay

If you work out your own tax, you also calculate your own payments on account for the next tax year. You should put this first payment in box 18.7 of the full tax return.

If HMRC works out your tax bill, it will send you a notice confirming your tax liability for the current tax year, and based on this, your payments on account for the following year. Contact HMRC straight away if you have queries.

## ❝If you work out your own tax, you also calculate your own payments on account.❞

## Asking for the tax to be taken from your pay packet or pension

The other option is asking HMRC to collect the tax via your PAYE code, providing the amount owed is less than £2,000. HMRC will guarantee to do this only if you file your tax return by 30 September (30 December if you file online).

If you don't want your underpaid tax deducted by PAYE, you must tick box 23.1 on your tax return.

## WHAT HAPPENS IF YOUR INCOME RISES OR FALLS

The self-assessment system works on a forward- and backward-looking principle. You pay half for the year in question but you have previously also paid forward the other half for the same year. And once you have paid one amount, you also pay towards the following tax year, which you have still to finish. The payment-on-account system assumes your tax affairs will remain the same from year to year. If your income (and tax bill) is rising, the payment on account will be less than you have to pay. But the opposite can often happen. It might be because you:

- Know your income will be lower – perhaps your self-employment is less profitable or you have lower savings and investment income.

 National Insurance Class 4 contributions are payed by the self-employed and are explained on page 57.

- Have more tax deducted at source by your employer or by changing your savings and investments.
- Have more tax allowances or reliefs – for example, becoming eligible for an age-related allowance (see page 10).

You can ask to cut your payments on account – that's the amount you have to pay towards the current year – if you think your tax bill for this year will be lower than the previous tax year. But you must be able to justify this.

## How to do it

If you calculate your own tax, tick box 18.6 on the main return (if you've already sent in your tax return, complete form SA303 to reduce payments on account). Put the new payment amount in box 18.7 of the main return and explain why you've reduced your payments in the 'Additional information' box 23.9.

If HMRC works out your tax, you should get a statement of account before the first payment is due, provided you have submitted your return by 30 September. This will contain an SA303 form, which you can use to reduce your payments. Alternatively, you can write to your tax office stating that you want to reduce your payments (giving a reason). If you file online, you can also make an online claim.

## Underpaying

If it turns out that you have underpaid tax having made a claim to reduce the level of your payments on account, you will have to pay interest on the difference. Interest is charged from the

Taxpayers who deliberately underpay by more than £25,000 face 'naming and shaming' under new rules introduced in 2009. Details of defaulters' names, addresses, trade profession or sector, and the amount of tax, interest and penalties levied will be published on the HMRC website where they will remain for one year. This is in addition to HMRC releasing details of those who are found guilty in criminal proceedings. Any taxpayer who makes a full unprompted disclosure of their defaults, or a prompted disclosure within a set time frame, will be exempt from the naming and shaming.

To contact the HMRC regarding queries on your self-assessment form, telephone: 0845 9000 444 (open 8am-8pm seven days a week).

date the payment was due – 31 January or 31 July. HMRC charges interest at a rate that generally moves up and down with the Bank of England base rate, although the date of any change may be delayed.

## Overpaying

If your payments on account are more than the tax you owe, you get interest on the difference. Again, interest is paid from the date the payment was due at a rate decided by HMRC. But this rate – while variable with interest rates in the economy – is far less than the amount HMRC charges if you have underpaid. However, it is tax free.

### WHEN YOUR FORM IS WRONG

HMRC receives over eight million tax forms a year. The vast bulk are dealt with by automated machinery – and most are correct. But a significant minority have errors. These fall into two main categories – those that HMRC considers minor and those that require more investigation.

## 'Repairing' your tax form

'Repairing' is HMRC-speak for putting minor errors right. These can include the items listed opposite.

- Not filling in the right pages – confusing employment with self-employment or putting down foreign income as UK income.

- Mixing up unit trusts and investment trusts.
- Confusing bank accounts with shares or vice versa – this happens a lot when people own shares in banks.
- Entering your monthly salary as your annual salary.
- Arithmetical errors, such as mistakes over percentages and decimal points.

Around half of these errors result in you over-paying and half in under-paying. Where the amounts are relatively small, HMRC will send you a note with the adjustments, which are usually small. Repairing is used for mistakes that are not considered deliberate.

## HMRC probes

More serious errors can result in a probe – officially known as an enquiry. There are a number of signals that set alarm bells ringing at HMRC, which include:

- Purposefully illegible forms or incomplete forms.
- Sending in forms very late – especially if you do this year after year.
- Forms that are wildly lower than a previous year with no obvious explanation.
- Forms largely or totally based on provisional figures rather than the actual numbers.
- People who live in very expensive houses (easily checked from the postcode and a number of home valuation websites) claiming to have little or no income.

- Where there is a discrepancy between what you tell HMRC and what you claim back from VAT.
- Self-employed people whose profits are substantially lower and expenses far higher than the average for the trade or profession (HMRC has access to information giving facts and figures on a large number of occupations – even down to the number of portions of chips a fish and chip shop can make from a given weight of potatoes).
- People in 'high-risk' groups, such as those dealing in the cash economy.

But HMRC can start an enquiry into anyone's forms. It does not have to explain why, but it does have to reveal which of the two types of enquiry it is. These are:

An aspect enquiry. This is limited to one part of the tax form – perhaps your capital gains or your buy-to-let business. It is the more common of the two probes. But an aspect enquiry can turn into a full enquiry.

In some circumstances, you can insure yourself against probes (see box, overleaf). You can also pay in money during the enquiry. This is not an admission of guilt but may help to mitigate any penalties you have to pay. Equally, owning up is always helpful!

A full enquiry. This is where HMRC looks into the whole of your return. This is the more serious of the two and is used when there is suspicion that large parts of your tax return (if you have bothered with one) are false. A full enquiry can go back over many years if there is a suspicion of serious fraud.

If you submit your return on time, HMRC normally has 12 months from the 31 January filing deadline to start an enquiry (so you'll be notified by 31 January 2011 for the 2008–9 return) and between 12 and 15 months from the date the return is actually filed. It must follow code of practice COP11. But these deadlines can be ignored if there is a suspicion of serious fraud.

At the end of the enquiry, you will either be told that you are in the clear – or you're not! But the 'enquiry closure notice' may detail penalties and interest

**"HMRC doesn't have to explain why it starts an enquiry, which could be limited or full, depending on the circumstances."**

To read COP11 'Self-assessment local office enquiries', go to www.hmrc.gov.uk/leaflets/cop11.pdf.

you have to pay. This is generally by agreement between the two sides. Prison is very rare – probably less than 100 cases in a typical year and many of those are also guilty of other offences.

**" An 'enquiry closure notice' may detail penalties and interest you have to pay. "**

## Insuring yourself against a tax investigation

A number of insurance brokers, accountancy firms (and other advisers who are involved in offering paid-for help with tax return filing) sell policies that pay additional accountancy fees if you are involved in a tax investigation or enquiry.

Every year, thousands are chosen at random to test the system – most are innocent of any wrongdoing. A larger number are selected for a fuller investigation from what HMRC considers 'risk categories' – traders who largely deal in cash items or who have a large number of difficult-to-explain overseas transactions are two examples.

These policies promise to pay any additional costs associated with a further enquiry or investigation, but your claim will not be met if the probe is down to suspected fraud. The policies will not pay any extra tax, interest, penalties and fines you might have to hand over. Nor can you buy one once HMRC has targeted you.

Expect to pay anything from £100 to £600 or more for a policy. But the cost has little connection with the cover. Many accountants buy the plans in bulk from specialist insurers and then sell them on to their customers for whatever they think their particular clientèle will be willing to pay.

# You and your tax rights

HMRC receives around 90,000 complaints a year – about three in every thousand taxpayers. Mistakes, delays and poor advice or customer service are common gripes, but they needn't be left unresolved. Whatever the problem, you have a right to complain if something goes wrong. This section explains your rights and how to complain.

## BASIC PROBLEMS

Whether your complaint concerns an unreasonable delay, a mistake that could have been avoided or poor or misleading advice, there is a formal complaints procedure you can follow.

1   Most difficulties are resolved with a phone call or, if it is more complicated, a letter. HMRC has service standards, which apply to the time it takes to answer a query or problem. But as these are target-driven, it is always hard to know whether your letter is the small percentage that fall outside the target. These targets vary from year to year but, typically, 80 per cent of postal queries should be dealt with within 15 days.

2   Complain to the officer in charge. Where a simple phone call or letter fails to resolve a service problem, you should first complain to the officer in charge of your local tax district or the district that deals with your affairs. HMRC has laid down standards of confidentiality and other matters in dealing with customers.

3   Consult leaflet IR120 'You and the Inland Revenue'. If complaining to the officer in charge fails to produce a satisfactory outcome, consult leaflet IR120, which tells you of the full complaints procedure. This involves escalating your problem to the director or controller with overall responsibility for that tax office.

4   Go to the revenue adjudicator's office. This is a last resort and you can also complain to your local member of parliament. The MP can raise the matter with the parliamentary ombudsman, although this is rare.

**❝ You have a right to complain if something goes wrong at HMRC. ❞**

## COMPLAINTS ABOUT THE AMOUNT OF TAX YOU HAVE TO PAY

If you disagree with a decision about the amount of tax you have to pay (whether it is Income Tax, Inheritance Tax, Capital Gains Tax or any other type of tax), you can normally appeal. The first step is to take up the matter with your local tax office. It may be a simple mistake or misunderstanding (on either side), which can easily be rectified.

But ultimately, you can take your case to an independent legal body, called the General or Special Commissioners. At this stage, you will probably also need professional help.

The first step is to write to HMRC at the address on the notice of decision, within 30 days of its date. Most problems are resolved at this stage, but if you find yourself locked in dispute, HMRC will pass your case to independent commissioners.

If you don't agree with the commissioners' decision, you have two further options.

**❝You can normally appeal if you disagree with a decision about the amount of tax to be paid.❞**

---

### Ask the expert

#### How do I know if I can appeal?

You can normally appeal against a decision, but if you are unsure, seek advice from your tax office or local enquiry centre. The General Commissioners can deal with most complaints, but if your case is particularly complicated or technical, it will normally be heard by the Special Commissioners (you or HMRC can also request this).

You can be represented at the hearing by someone else, but this may be refused if the person isn't a lawyer or accountant. There are no fees for making an appeal to the commissioners, although costs may be awarded. However, appealing to the High Court/Court of Session/Court of Appeal can be costly if you lose, as HMRC may seek to recover their costs from you.

---

 For contact details for the adjudicator's office and Parliamentary ombudsman, see Useful addresses on pages 212-13.

- If there was an administrative error that affected the decision, or you couldn't attend the hearing, or the commissioners didn't see all of the relevant information, you can ask the commissioners to review their decision.
- **If you think the decision is wrong on a point of law,** you can appeal to the High Court (Court of Session in Scotland, Court of Appeal in Northern Ireland).

There are no fees for making an appeal to the commissioners. However, appealing to the High Court/Court of Session/Court of Appeal can be very costly if you lose as HMRC may seek to recover their costs from you.

## When you can claim compensation

You may be able to claim back reasonable costs that you've incurred as a direct result of HMRC mistakes or delays. These might include:

- Postage
- Phone calls
- Travelling expenses necessary with your claim
- Professional fees, such as accountancy and legal bills.

Additionally, if the mistakes or delays have caused you a lot of worry or inconvenience, or if your complaint was handled badly or if HMRC took an unreasonable time to deal with it, you may also be able to claim compensation for your distress. These payments usually range from £25 to £500.

## Tax overpayments

If this is the fault of HMRC, you should complain and then claim compensation in line with that detailed above.

Where you made a mistake in your return (by over-declaring income) or where you failed to claim an allowance to which you were entitled, you can claim a

**❝ If tax overpayment is a fault of HMRC, complain and then claim compensation. These payments usually range from £25 to £500. ❞**

 It is your responsibility to read carefully the relevant notices and to check that the tax due has been calculated on the basis of correct information. In many cases, complaints aren't upheld by tax inspectors, or finally by the adjudicator, as complainants haven't taken notice of instructions and guidance.

repayment within five years of the filing date of the tax return following the end of the relevant tax year. This means you have until 31 January 2011 to claim for the 2004–5 tax year.

## Tax underpayments

HMRC will sometimes pursue you for unpaid tax. You have to pay this (usually with penalties and interest) if this is your fault. But where HMRC miscalculated or ignored correct information provided by you, your employer or any benefits payer, you can ask it not to pursue any underpaid tax. The same applies if it repays you too much tax and then asks for some of it back.

Issues concerning tax codes and underpaid tax continue to be one of the main areas of complaint dealt with by the adjudicator. However, tax will normally be written off only where:

- **You were notified of arrears more than a year** after the end of the tax year in which HMRC received the relevant information – this is unfair as you have the right to assume (when you have filled in the form correctly) that once your assessment has been issued, that is the end of it. Moreover, with the exception of records from self-employment, you only have to keep your records for one year after the final date for sending in the self-assessment form – the requirement for keeping records for the 2008–9 tax year (other than self-employment) is to hold them until 31 January 2011.

- **You were notified of the overpayment** after the end of the tax year following the year in which the repayment was made.

- **You could have reasonably believed** you had paid the right amount of tax.

## FINDING YOUR TAX OFFICE

Your tax office is determined by your employment status.

### If you are an employee/ your main income is a pension from a former employer

Your tax office is determined by the location of the main office of your employer or whoever pays your pension. This may not be anywhere near the employer or pension payer, however. Many central London tax districts are dealt with in Scotland.

> **"If you underpay and it is your fault, you will have to pay the balance to HMRC."**

For more information, see the HMRC guide: 'Tax appeals: a guide to appealing against decisions of the Inland Revenue on tax and other matters'.

## Tax tip

You can always ask for a face-to-face meeting, if necessary, at a tax office convenient for you, such as one near your home or workplace. You will have to make an appointment so any documents required can be available.

some north-west London tax offices were moved to Devon along with the documentation for many hundreds of thousands of London inhabitants.

## If you are unemployed
You remain with your previous tax office.

## If you are self-employed
You will be dealt with by a 'local' tax office. But this could be hundreds of miles from your home – for instance,

**❝ A 'local' tax office can be hundreds of miles away from your home. ❞**

## Ask the expert

### I'm in employment. How do I find the details of my tax office?

If you work for an organisation and have tax deducted through PAYE, you will normally find that all employees have the same tax office, no matter where they are from. The tax office may also have no geographical relationship to any of the locations where your firm is based – for instance a company whose employees are divided equally between Manchester and London could have a tax office in Scotland.

To find out, start by asking your payroll or personnel department, who should give you the reference number, address and phone number of the relevant tax office.

In some companies, you may also find the details on your payslip - they should certainly be on the P60 that you receive at the end of the tax year, or on the P45 you receive when you leave the company.

Small firms normally have their affairs dealt with by the local tax office although that does not always mean the office is conveniently local! HMRC have shut a number of offices and moved the work to cheaper premises elsewhere.

# The Taxpayers' Charter

At the time of writing, consultation was continuing (as it has done for the past five years) on revising the Taxpayers' Charter, the original version of which dates back to 1986. As with all codes and charters, this is voluntary and not binding in law. However, it is a point of reference for both sides, enabling taxpayer and HMRC to start with a framework governing the solution of problems. A new version is due to be published in late 2009 or in 2010, but here is a brief summary of the current charter.

## Your rights

- HMRC promises to treat you with courtesy and consideration at all times and will, in normal circumstances, strive to help you to understand and meet your tax obligations, explain reasons for decisions, finalise refund requests speedily and, where the law allows, pay you interest on the amount.
- There are also standards for replies to written enquiries, answering the phone, keeping your costs down and detailing how amounts are calculated.

## Your rights of appeal

This details how HMRC should:

- Explain your rights of review, objection and appeal if you are unsure of them or need clarification.
- Review your case if you believe that it has misinterpreted facts, applied the law incorrectly or not handled your affairs properly.
- Ensure the review is completed in a comprehensive, professional and impartial manner by a representative from HMRC who has not been involved in the original decision, and give an answer to your objection as quickly as possible.

There are also rights to know the tax implications of what you do. You should be told (if you ask) of the effect of any change in your earnings or in the way those earnings are made up (although you cannot get individual advice as to whether a particular course is right or not for you). You also have a right to privacy (this ensures HMRC has to take care with your personal and private data) and to be treated considerately if you have to have an interview or further investigation into your affairs.

**"** The Taxpayers' Charter is not binding in law, but it is a point of reference for both sides as it provides a framework governing the solution of problems. **"**

## Your right to certainty

HMRC says that in normal circumstances, they will strive to:

- Provide you with advice about the tax implications of your actions.
- Let you know [at least ... days]/[as soon as possible] before the conduct of an interview or a request for the production of documents.
- Advise you of the scope of an interview and their requirements.
- Arrange a suitable time and place for the interview and allow you time to prepare your records.

## Your obligations

Under the charter, the taxpayer has an obligation to:

- Be honest.
- Provide complete and accurate information as and when required.
- Pay taxes on time.
- Keep records.
- Be co-operative.

 For more information about the Taxpayers' Charter, go to  www.taxpayerscharter. co.uk/content/view/72/27/.

# Getting outside help

There is a wide variety of help available for taxpayers ranging from £1,000-an-hour accountants to a unique charity that can help with your tax affairs. This section tells you more.

## PAID-FOR SERVICES

There are a number of different ways of paying for help with filing your tax return. These can be useful if you need professional advice, have complicated tax affairs or simply don't have the time to do it yourself. The hourly rates are estimated ranges – you could pay more or less. Whatever their professional qualifications or their charging rate, all are known to HMRC as 'tax agents'. Paid-for services include the following personnel.

## Chartered accountants

These are registered either with the Institute of Chartered Accountants in England and Wales or the Institute of Chartered Accountants in Scotland.

**ʕʕ If you use a tax agent, you will still have to take legal responsibility. ʔʔ**

Chartered accountants tend to be the most expensive but cover the widest range of services. They include very large City firms, which advise on multi-billion deals. Not all are interested in dealing with personal or small business tax affairs.

Expect to pay anything from £70 to £1,000 an hour – plus VAT. Typically, someone with a full-time job, some investments and savings and small self-employment earnings would expect to pay £250–£350 for help with their tax return.

## Chartered certified accountants

These tend to be smaller firms, often specialising in individual or small business affairs. Expect to pay from £50 to £250 an hour – plus VAT. Relatively simple returns tend to cost £200–£300.

## Form checkers

A number of banks, building societies and a few specialist firms offer a form

Details of members of the Institute of Chartered Accountants, their services and complaints procedures can be found on www.icaew.co.uk. For the Association of Chartered Certified Accountants, go to www.accaglobal.com.

checking service, which is designed to ensure you pay the right amount and get the self-assessment return in on time, avoiding penalties. You provide them with information such as your earnings and interest income. They usually limit themselves to simple personal tax affairs, so they are rarely suitable if you have some self-employment or other complications, such as rental income or overseas income. They should point out mistakes, but you will not generally get individual advice on reducing your tax bill. Expect to pay £100–£150 for the basic service. Some will offer to look at past tax returns to see if there is anything you could still claim for – often on a no-win, no-fee basis where they take a pre-agreed percentage of anything they recover for you.

## Rebate companies

These are specialised firms that concentrate on tax rebates for people who have worked in the UK for a short time – typically foreign students and

## Get it in writing

Whatever level of paid-for advice you opt for, always make sure that you have a clear statement beforehand of what will be provided, what you will be expected to provide, how much you will be asked to pay for the service, and how (and when) any rebate will be paid to you.

**" If your tax affairs are simple, consider using a form checking service from a bank or building society. "**

## Tax tip

If you are self-employed (or in a business partnership), you can claim the cost of professional costs, including accountancy and legal fees, so you effectively reduce your profits (or increase your losses). If you are VAT-registered, you can reclaim the VAT on the fees. Both the VAT and the Income Tax relief is limited to the costs involved in sorting out your business affairs – you cannot claim accountancy fees in relation to your non-business affairs, such as your savings and investments.

'backpackers' – who have had tax deducted but who are owed a rebate because they did not earn enough in a tax year to pay UK Income Tax.

Rebate companies typically charge 25–40 per cent of the amount they recover – usually on a no-win, no-fee basis. They can go back six years. But they can only work on what they receive – they will not go to past employers to find out information on your behalf. You can, of course, apply for your own rebate and pay nothing.

## DOING SOME OF THE WORK YOURSELF

You can save a considerable amount of money if you provide your accountant or other hired help with all the facts (or as many as possible), such as a list of the dividends you received, any profits or losses made on investments and also how much interest your savings will have gained.

If you are running a business, then looking at the headings of what you can claim as expenses (see pages 64–5) and what you have to declare as income will enable you to provide figures that would otherwise be costly to obtain.

Accountants will often charge the same per hour whether it is sorting out a shoe box full of jumbled paperwork or providing high-level advice.

**❝ You can save yourself money by keeping good records of your expenses and what you declare as income. ❞**

 To contact TaxAid, go to www.taxaid.org.uk or the helpline is open 10am–12 noon, Monday–Thursday.

# FREE SERVICES

You don't always have to pay for tax help – even if the problem is complex. There are sources of free information plus no-cost help for the less well off.

## TaxAid

This is a unique charity that offers free, independent and confidential advice to anyone on a low income who has a tax question or problem and cannot afford a tax professional. It is financed by a number of bodies, including the National Lottery.

TaxAid sets out to help you understand your rights and responsibilities under the UK tax system (including the information HMRC has sent you about your tax), on matters such as PAYE, self-assessment, Tax Credits and allowances and tax for the self-employed.

TaxAid can also help:

- If you are the subject of an HMRC probe
- When you cannot pay the tax that is due and may be facing legal proceedings, including bankruptcy for non-payment
- Where you think you should get a tax refund
- Where you feel you are being unfairly treated by HMRC.

All TaxAid advisers are qualified tax professionals.

# Glossary

**Allowances:** Technical term for the first slice of earnings or of capital gains or an inheritance, which is free of tax.

**Benefit in kind:** A perk, such as a company car or private medical insurance, provided by an employer instead of salary.

**Bonds:** These allow governments, international bodies and companies to borrow, usually for a fixed time at a fixed annual dividend rate. Traded on the stock market.

**Capital allowances:** Accounting term for the proportion of a major expenditure item, such as a machine or computer, which can be offset against tax.

**Capital Gains Tax (CGT):** A tax on profits made when selling items – most commonly, shares and second homes.

**Cash basis accounting:** Recording sales and expenses only when cash is received or paid out, rather than when you send invoices or receive bills. Used by small businesses.

**Chargeable transfer:** A transfer from one person to another not exempt from Inheritance Tax. You must notify HMRC of any such transfer worth over £200,000.

**Child Tax Credit (CTC):** An annual sum – currently £545 – paid to families with incomes up to £58,000 a year (up to £66,000 if a child is under one).

**Child Trust Fund (CTF):** A tax-free savings scheme that is started with government money. It can only be encashed when the child reaches 18 years of age.

**Consumer prices index:** The Government's preferred measure of rising prices. It includes most goods but excludes Council Tax and housing costs.

**Corporate bonds:** Bonds from companies in the UK and elsewhere. They often pay a higher rate of return compared to bonds from governments.

**Dispensation:** A formal agreement between an employer and HMRC allowing certain expenses to be paid tax free.

**Dividend:** Regular payment from shares.

**Emolument:** Tax-talk for what you earn from employment.

**Enterprise Investment Scheme (EIS):** A government-approved scheme offering tax relief to investors in small, and often risky, companies not quoted on the stock market.

**Equities:** *See* Shares.

**Equity release scheme:** A plan where you hand over your property or part of it on death to a financial firm in return for an immediate lump sum or a regular lifetime income.

**ES40 booklet:** Issued when you return to work after a long period away from paid employment.

**Excise duties:** Taxes on goods such as alcohol, tobacco and petrol.

**Film finance plans:** Complex tax schemes aimed at the wealthy backing UK film productions.

**Flexible benefits:** A 'menu' of employer benefits, such as extra holidays or private medical insurance, which employees can mix and match up to a maximum amount agreed with the employer.

**Friendly society:** Life insurer that is allowed to issue tax-free investment plans.

**Gift Aid:** Enables donations to charity with tax relief.

**Gifts with reservation of benefit:** The giver retains the right either to use it or ask for it back without payment or at a non-commercial rate.

**Gilts (short for gilt-edged securities):** British government bonds.

**Incapacity Benefit:** A long-term sickness benefit.

**Income Support:** A means-tested benefit for those below State Pension age who are out of work or ill.

**Individual Savings Account (ISA):** Tax-free way of saving in shares or bank/building society accounts.

**Inheritance Tax (IHT):** Paid on the estates of those who die.

**Investment trust:** A company whose sole purpose is to invest in a basket of shares from other companies.

**Jobseeker's Allowance:** A non-means-tested benefit for those out of work but actively looking for a job.

**Local authority fixed-interest investments:** Loans issued by UK local authorities, paying a fixed interest rate for a set period.

**National Insurance:** A tax that gives some benefits to the contributor, including the State Pension and Jobseeker's Allowance.

**National Insurance credits:** Given to those who cannot work because of family responsibilities, sickness or unemployment.

**National Insurance surcharge:** The 1 per cent extra levied on higher earners. It offers no benefits.

**Net income:** What is left over after all tax deductions have been made from your earnings.

**Overlap:** Where the accounting year you have chosen and the official tax year do not coincide – it can mean complicated and sometimes higher tax bills when you start out.

**P45 form:** Received when you leave a job. You take the form to your new employer to ensure continuity of PAYE deductions.

**P46 form:** A form that you take to a new employer if you have never worked before or if you have been out of the workforce during the whole of the tax year when you start the new job.

Pay As You Earn (PAYE): Method of taking tax from regular salaries.

Payments on account: Amounts you pay HMRC via your self-assessment form for future periods – even though you have not yet earned them.

Payroll giving: Deductions from salary that go to charity.

Permanent income-bearing shares (PIBS): A building society investment with a fixed interest rate, but without a guaranteed final repayment date.

Personal Allowance: The amount of income that you can have each tax year without having to pay Income Tax.

Potentially exempt transfer (PET): A gift free of IHT, provided the donor lives seven years after making a gift.

R85 form: Used at banks and building societies to declare the account holder is a non-taxpayer.

Rent-a-Room Scheme: Allows you to earn up to £4,250 a year from a lodger in your home tax free.

Salary sacrifice/Sacrifice scheme: Giving up part of your salary in return for benefits with Income Tax or National Insurance advantages.

Save As You Earn (SAYE): Regular savings plan that enables you to take a share stake in your employer's company.

Self-assessment tax return: A form that about one-in-three taxpayers fill in each year – usually those who will owe tax greater than what is taken from their pay packet.

Self-Invested Personal Pension (SIPP): A plan where you control the investment content – you can include a wide variety of assets but not residential property.

Shares (also known as equities): These give holders the right to dividends and a say in the company's running – in proportion to the amount of shares they hold. Shares are traded on the stock market and can rise or fall.

Stakeholder Pension: A government-backed scheme to provide low-cost personal pension plans. All employers with five or more staff have to offer one to their workforce but no employer is obliged to contribute to the plan.

Stamp duty: A 0.5 per cent tax on most share purchases.

Stamp duty land tax: A tax on property purchase.

Statutory maternity, paternity or adoption pay: Taxable cash from the state when you are off work due to pregnancy and childbirth or a legal adoption – paid when you do not receive a minimum amount from an employer.

Statutory sick pay: Taxable payment from the state when you are off work due to illness – it is only paid if your employer does not continue paying you.

Tax code: A number and a letter that tells your employer exactly how much Income Tax to deduct from your pay packet.

Tax year: The Income Tax year starts on 6 April each year and ends on 5 April – it has nothing to do with the self-assessment timetable.

Taxable income: The amount of income that you have left after your Personal Allowance and pension contributions have been taken from your earnings, which is then taxed.

Top slicing: A tax calculation used when encashing with profits and other insurance bonds.

Trust fund: Assets controlled by one person on behalf of another – typically a child.

Unit trust (officially known as an open-ended investment company (OEIC)): An investment in a basket of shares so investors can spread equity-owning risks.

Value Added Tax (VAT): Percentage added to many goods and services we purchase. Can be reclaimed by VAT registered traders.

Venture Capital Trust (VCT): Allows investors to spread risks across a basket of small and start-up company shares with tax relief.

Voluntary agreement: A deal whereby your employer agrees to pick up the tax bill on expenses otherwise taxable such as entertaining clients, where the cost of the employee's meal should be taxable.

Working Tax Credit (WTC): A pay packet boost through the tax system for employees and the self-employed on low earnings.

# Useful addresses

## England and Wales

The Adjudicator's Office
Haymarket House
28 Haymarket
London SW1Y 4SP
Tel: 0300 057 1111
www.adjudicatorsoffice.gov.uk

Association of Chartered Certified
Accountants (ACCA)
(to find an accountant)
2 Central Quay
89 Hydepark Street
Glasgow G3 8BW
Tel: 0141 582 2000
www.acca.co.uk

The Chartered Institute of Taxation
(to find a tax adviser)
12 Upper Belgrave Street
London SW1X 8BB
Tel: 020 7235 9381
www.tax.org.uk

Department for Work and Pensions
www.dwp.gov.uk (see website for all local
office phone numbers)

Future Pension Centre
The Pension Service
Tyneview Park
Whitley Road
Newcastle upon Tyne NE98 1BA

HM Revenue & Customs (HMRC)
- For local tax enquiry centres look in
  *The Phone Book* under 'HM Revenue &
  Customs'
- For your local tax office, check your tax
  return, other tax correspondence or check
  with your employer
- HMRC Orderline (IHT): 0845 234 1000
- HMRC Orderline (self-assessment):
  0845 9000 404
- HMRC Orderline (taxback for non-
  taxpayers): 0845 9000 444
- Business anti-fraud line: 0800 854 440
- Website: www.hmrc.gov.uk
- Child Trust Fund website:
  www.childtrustfund.gov.uk

HMRC Inheritance Tax
Ferrers House
Castle Meadow Road
Nottingham NG2 1BB
Inheritance Tax helpline: 0845 302 0900
www.hmrc.gov.uk/cto/iht.htm

Institute of Chartered Accountants in
England and Wales
(to find an accountant)
PO Box 433
Chartered Accountants' Hall
Moorgate Place
London EC2R 6EA
Tel: 020 7920 8100
www.icaew.co.uk

Jobcentre Plus
Tel: 0800 055 6688 (Monday to Friday,
8am–6pm)
www.jobcentreplus.gov.uk

**National Insurance Contributions Office**
*(for National Insurance contributions)*
Benton Park View
Newcastle upon Tyne NE98 1ZZ
Tel: 0845 302 1479 (Monday to Friday,
8am–5pm)
www.hmrc.gov.uk/nic/offices.htm

**The Parliamentary and Health Service
Ombudsman**
Office of the Parliamentary Commissioner
for Administration
Millbank Tower
Millbank
London SW1P 4QP
Tel: 0345 015 4033 (Monday to Friday,
8.30am–5.30pm)
www.ombudsman.org.uk

**The Pension Service**
Tel: 0845 6060265
www.thepensionservice.gov.uk

# Northern Ireland

**Department for Social Development in
Northern Ireland**
*(for benefits and pensions)*
www.dsdni.gov.uk (see website for all local
office phone numbers)

HMRC Inheritance Tax
Level 3
Dorchester House
52–58 Great Victoria Street
Belfast BT2 7QL
www.hmrc.gov.uk

**Institute of Chartered Accountants in
Ireland**
*(to find an accountant)*
The Linenhall
32–38 Linenhall Street
Belfast BT2 8BG
Tel: 028 9032 1600
www.icai.ie

# Scotland

HMRC Inheritance Tax
Meldrum House
15 Drumsheugh Gardens
Edinburgh EH3 7UG
Tel: 0845 234 1000 (for forms and
leaflets)
www.hmrc.gov.uk

**Institute of Chartered Accountants of
Scotland**
*(to find an accountant)*
CA House
21 Haymarket Yards
Edinburgh EH12 5BH
Tel: 0131 347 0100
www.icas.org.uk

# Index

**217**

Index

## Which? Books

### Other books in this series

### Finance Your Retirement
Jonquil Lowe
ISBN: 978 1 84490 057 2
Price £10.99

*Finance Your Retirement* is the essential step-by-step guide to a secure retirement, providing advice on saving for your pension, whether to opt for an annuity, how to access your money if you retire abroad and the basics of Inheritance Tax. There are helpful tips for maximising your budget using state benefits and investments, such as unit trusts and OEICs, plus guidance on how to make your property work for you.

### Managing Your Debt
Phillip Inman
ISBN: 978 1 84490 041 1
Price £10.99

*Managing Your Debt* is a practical and straightforward guide to managing your finances and getting your money, and your life, back on track. Phillip Inman, the *Guardian*'s business correspondent covers a wide range of topics including how to identify and deal with priority debts, the best way to make a debt-management plan, who to contact and what to expect should you ever face bankruptcy or an individual voluntary agreement.

### Money Saving Handbook
Tony Levene
ISBN: 978 1 84490 048 0
Price £10.99

From low-cost air travel and zero per cent finance to cheap mobile phone tariffs, the list of financial products is endless and the good deals are harder to find. Personal finance expert, Tony Levene, separates the cons from the bargains and explains how to avoid hidden charges and penalty fees. *Money Saving Handbook* is the key to becoming smarter with your money.

## Which? Books

### Other books in this series

#### The Bright Idea Handbook
Michael Gardner
ISBN: 978 1 84490 059 6
Price £10.99

There can be many hurdles on the road to commercial success, from asserting your rights as creator, through to getting the funding and market launch you need. *The Bright Idea Handbook* provides practical, step-by-step guidance for understanding intellectual property law and how to protect it. It also outlines how to pitch for finance, plan your advertising and marketing strategy and get distribution of your product or service up and running. If you have a bright idea waiting to be explored, this is the book for you!

#### Baby and Toddler Essentials
Anne Smith
ISBN: 978 1 84490 035 0
Price £10.99

Knowing what you need to buy for a child can be a daunting business. The choice is huge and the advice from parenting magazines and websites can often be overwhelming. How do you weigh up the manufacturers' claims and make the right choices for you and the little one? Packed with tips on what to look for and what to avoid, *Baby and Toddler Essentials* is an indispensable guide for parents, grandparents and carers.

#### Working for Yourself
Mike Pywell and Bill Hilton
ISBN: 978 1 84490 040 4
Price £10.99

Most of us want the freedom offered by self-employment. *Working for Yourself* will help you make that jump out of the rat race. Covering tips on freelancing, consultancy and contract work, this book provides all the financial and legal information to get you off to the best start possible.

# Which? Books

## Other books in this series

### Develop Your Property
Kate Faulkner
ISBN: 978 1 84490 038 1
Price £10.99

*Develop Your Property* is aimed at the thousands of people in the UK who are looking to make a serious and long-term investment in their property. Covering planning permission and building regulations, this guide deals with property development in a jargon-free and unbiased manner.

### NEW EDITION
### Renting and Letting
Kate Faulkner
ISBN: 978 1 84490 054 1
Price £10.99

A practical guide for landlords, tenants and anybody considering the buy-to-let market. Written by an experienced property professional, this real-world guide covers all the legal and financial matters, including tax, record-keeping and mortgages, as well as disputes and security. This new edition features the latest on energy performance certificates and tenancy deposit protection schemes.

### Save and Invest
Jonquil Lowe
ISBN: 978 1 84490 044 2
Price £10.99

*Save and Invest* is a detailed guide to all saving and investment avenues suitable for those approaching the markets for the first time and those seeking to improve their portfolio. Jonquil Lowe, an experienced investment analyst, introduces the basics of understanding risk and suggests popular starter investments. Many types of savings accounts are closely analysed, along with more complex investment options, such as venture capital trusts, high-income bonds, hedge funds and spread betting.

## Which? Books

Which? Books provide impartial, expert advice on everyday matters from finance to law, property to major life events. We also publish the country's most trusted restaurant guide, *The Good Food Guide*. To find out more about Which? Books, log on to www.which.co.uk or call 01903 828557.

**❝**Which? tackles the issues that really matter to consumers and gives you the advice and active support you need to buy the right products.**❞**